LOCAL GOVERNMENT EXPLAINED

LOCAL GOVERNMENT EXPLAINED

Ivor H. Seeley

B.Sc., M.A., Ph.D., F.R.I.C.S., C.Eng.,
F.I.Mun.E., F.I.Q.S., M.I.O.B.

*Head of the Department of Surveying
and Dean of the School of Environmental Studies,
Trent Polytechnic, Nottingham*

First edition 1978
Reprinted 1983

Published by
THE MACMILLAN PRESS LTD
London and Basingstoke
Companies and representatives
throughout the world

Printed in Hong Kong

British Library Cataloguing in Publication Data

Seeley, Ivor Hugh
Local government explained.
1.   Local government – Great Britain
I.   Title
352.041   JS3025

ISBN 0–333–22355–1
ISBN 0–333–22357–8   Pbk

This book is dedicated to the councillors of the former urban district of Haverhill and the former rural district of Newport Pagnell, with whom I had the privilege to be associated as a chief officer.

CONTENTS

minutes; local government staffing: the local government service, conditions of employment, personnel management, superannuation, conditions of service; recruitment and training: recruitment, induction, training, Local Government Training Board; staff development: selection, promotion and career prospects, manpower planning; references

Financial needs of local authorities: budgets; main sources of local government income; rating: nature and method of operation, valuations and valuation lists, merits and demerits of rating, rate rebates and other forms of assistance, reforms; financial relations with central government: grants, subsidies, loans; financial problems of local authorities in the mid-1970s; alternative sources of local authority income: local income tax, local sales tax, local employment or payroll tax, motor fuel duty, motor vehicle duties, super-rating, surcharges on rates for earning non-householders, site value rating, rating of agriculture, lotteries; Layfield Report and the future in local government finance; references

General powers: Statutory Instruments; doctrine of *ultra vires*; judicial control; Acts of Parliament: public Acts, private Acts, Clauses Acts; Orders; bye-laws: nature and scope, making of bye-laws, confirmation of bye-laws, model bye-laws, validity of bye-laws, relaxation and re-approval of bye-laws; legal status of local authorities; local authorities in litigation, Commissioners for Local Administration; references

Central and local government relationships; legislative control; administrative control: general powers, directions, regulations, bye-laws, supervision, inspection, other ministerial actions and requirements, central–local communications; financial control: loans, grants; district audit: nature and form of audit, appointment and duties of auditors, district audit procedure, advantages of district audit; appeals, default powers and settlement of disputes; control through inspection: inspection of services, inspectorate and inquiries; approval of schemes; effect of central control; references

LIST OF FIGURES

LIST OF TABLES

PREFACE

This book is aimed primarily at students of local government, whatever their discipline, but may also be of value to new and prospective councillors and officers, and to members of the public who are interested in the workings of local government.

After delving into the foundations of local government, the changes to the local government structure and functions are examined, followed by an analysis of operative procedures and techniques. The sources of finance, their deficiencies and alternative arrangements are explored, together with the powers and responsibilities of local authorities and the form and extent of central government control. Finally, current local government needs are investigated and an eye directed at the future.

Most of my career has been spent in the local government service, including some six years as a chief officer. I am proud to have served an important branch of the public service which has done so much to improve the health, comfort, well-being and education of the citizens of this country.

Views diverge widely as to the optimum local government structure for the United Kingdom and it has, sadly, become a political issue. Present experience points to the undesirability of sharing functions between different tiers and of separating interrelated activities which ought desirably to be grouped within the same authority. Some flexibility is needed as a single framework cannot be applied effectively to the whole country. Finally, a proper balance must be achieved between efficiency and democracy.

Relationships between officers and members and between central and local government need to be deeply rooted in respect and understanding one for the other. Local government would benefit from greater freedom of action and increased scope for the exercise of initiative in responding to local needs and aspirations. If local authorities were merely to become the agents of central government, it would be the end of effective and democratic local government and the country would be the poorer for it.

The operation of the local government service is dependent upon thousands of devoted elected members, who give selflessly of their time and energy in the interests of the community. As local government activities become increasingly complex they draw ever more

heavily upon councillors' time and it may become necessary in
the future to pay salaries to some, if not all, councillors. Any
corruption occurring in local government is given maximum
publicity by the media, whereas the total number of serious cases
of fraud or corruption is comparatively small, giving testimony
to the integrity of the vast majority of people connected with the
local government service, despite the many temptations they face.

The nineteen-seventies have seen a substantial increase in the
degree of involvement of party politics in local government. Where
all decisions are made by a political group outside council and
committee meetings, with little or no opportunity for discussion
or debate, healthy and democratic local government can easily
be undermined.

The mid-nineteen-seventies have shown the vulnerability of local
authorities in times of economic crisis, with such a high proportion
of their funds obtained from central sources. The problem is
accentuated by central government delegating new and costly
activities to local authorities at the same time as it is reducing local
government grants.

Improved and closer working arrangements between local
authorities and the press are needed. Local authorities must allow
ample access to the press and the public, while the press must
endeavour to report accurately and fully. Local authorities have
an important public relations function and should aim to keep
the public well informed of their proposals, problems and
achievements.

I would like to acknowledge the help I have received from
NALGO Education Department in the supply of valuable information, the *Local Government Chronicle* and Clifford Smith, Chief Executive
to Suffolk County Council, for supplying the basic data for Figure
7, and the Controller of Her Majesty's Stationery Office for permission to incorporate extracts from Government reports. For the legal
background I have drawn freely upon the well established and
authoritative works of C. A. Cross and W. O. Hart. Charles Hardwick
of the Trent Polytechnic Library provided a wealth of supporting
information and data.

Other fruitful sources of information were the numerous journals
impinging upon local government, and particularly *Local Government
Chronicle, Local Government Review, Municipal Review, Local Government
Studies, Public Finance and Accountancy* and *Local Government Annotations*.

I am indebted to all the officers and councillors who over the
years have given me the benefit of their views and experience, for
which I have been much the richer and wiser. It is on occasions
beneficial for the enthusiasm of officers to be moderated by experi-

enced elected members, whose primary aim is to satisfy pressing local needs within the available resources.

Finally, I have used the term 'Minister' extensively to cover the Secretary of State for the Environment.

Nottingham   IVOR H. SEELEY
Autumn 1977

CHAPTER ONE

HISTORICAL DEVELOPMENT OF LOCAL GOVERNMENT

Early Developments

A study of local government would not be complete without at least a cursory glance at the early beginnings of this vital system – the provision, operation and maintenance of essential public services at local level.

Richards[1] has described how the three traditional units of local government in England and Wales have been the county, the parish and the borough, each possessing a considerable degree of independence. Central interference with local institutions varied over time but these institutions were generally allowed to attend to local needs in the manner which they believed best, largely because of the poor communications and restricted resources in earlier times. National grants were not available until the 1840s and hence the scale of local activities was restricted. This resulted in the establishment of new or *ad hoc* bodies to provide services which the traditional authorities were unable or unwilling to offer.

Mediaeval Period

During the Middle Ages the country, being predominantly agricultural with a widely scattered population, was divided into counties. Each county was administered by a county court made up of freemen of the shire and presided over by the sheriff appointed by the Crown. Hart and Garner[2] have emphasised that these courts were more akin to governmental assemblies than judicial bodies.

Each county was divided into hundreds, of which there were about 700 in all, each administered by a hundred court. At a lower level came the vill or township without a court, which constituted a rudimentary police authority, and the manor, which was concerned primarily with agricultural matters. Largely outside county jurisdiction were the boroughs; they engaged in trade and commerce and possessed certain privileges, some being granted by royal charters. The boroughs enjoyed separate parliamentary representation from the counties.

The voting of money for church purposes was the function of all parishioners meeting in the vestry, using churchwardens as their officers. The parish was later to acquire non-ecclesiastical functions.

Tudor Period

The mediaeval system of local government based upon the sheriff and the county, hundred and manor courts fell into disuse and, in the first instance, most of the duties were undertaken by justices of the peace appointed by the Crown on their circuits around the country. The King's justices prevented the growth of power of nobles who might have threatened the unity of the kingdom.[3]

New social and economic problems accompanied the growth of industry in the sixteenth century. The enclosure of common fields resulted in many unemployed serfs who urgently needed relief, and the dissolution of the monasteries by Henry VIII abolished a valuable source of poor relief. Increased commerce produced the need for a better system of road maintenance.

To meet these needs local government was reorganised on the basis of the parish with Justices of the Peace undertaking a co-ordinating and controlling role. A considerable body of new legislation followed. By the Statute of Highways 1555, each parish had to appoint two surveyors responsible for the repair of roads in the parish, and the inhabitants were required to devote four days' labour a year to the maintenance work. Wealthier persons could pay a highway rate in lieu of work, and this money was used to pay the poor working on the roads. The administrative duties of the parish were greatly increased by the Poor Relief Act 1601. Each parish had to appoint an overseer who recovered a rate from local inhabitants for the purchase of materials on which the poor could work. It seldom proved practicable to provide the work and it was largely replaced by the distribution of relief financed by a parish rate. Hence each parish carried out its duties through four categories of unpaid officer – overseer of the poor, surveyor, constable and churchwarden.[1]

The Eighteenth Century

Central administrative control over Justices of the Peace ceased after the Revolution of 1688. Quarter sessions operated as the principal link between central and local administration. This body consisted of all the county Justices of Peace and met at least four times a year. When dealing with administrative matters, quarter sessions followed judicial procedure in the early part of the century. Later the approach changed when the Justices adjourned into a private meeting to discuss 'county business', following the judicial work. The number of county officers increased, they attended the quarterly meetings and were largely responsible for the execution of the decisions.

The eighteenth century saw the establishment of various *ad hoc* authorities each providing a specific service within a particular area whose boundaries might not coincide with those of other authorities. Problems were caused by concentrations of population and the corrupt and inefficient organisation of many boroughs. Hence local Acts created improvement commissioners to undertake such duties as paving, watching, lighting, street-cleansing and general improvements, financed through rates. Other local Acts authorised the establishment of corporations to take over poor relief functions from the unpaid parochial overseers. In like manner turnpike trustees were charged with maintaining existing main roads and providing new ones, and were empowered to levy tolls on road users.[2]

Position in Early Nineteenth Century

Parishes

In 1832 there were over 15 000 parishes, each being a distinctive unit of local administration but varying considerably in area, population and the number and method of appointment of officials.[3] The parishes in towns and cities exercised important functions in common with rural parishes.

All inhabitants had a right to participate in parochial business and a duty to carry out, in turn, the duties of parochial offices. In practice arrangements for the administration of the parish reflected its economic and social order, and open parish vestries were often a small oligarchy of intimate neighbours presided over by the clergyman or senior churchwarden and dominated by neighbouring Justices of the Peace.[4]

In rural communities there was much less abuse of the vestry system than in towns, as most inhabitants were known to each other. The close or select vestries which became established lent themselves to corrupt practices by consisting of a restricted number of people (10 to 24) serving for life and filling vacancies by co-option. There was also an unhealthy tendency for those who did not want to serve to pay to be excused, and for those who did serve to require some reward. On occasions an unscrupulous person took control of the local administration to his own advantage.

The Sturge Bourne Acts of 1818 and 1819 made the first changes in the legal constitution of the parishes. They introduced a property qualification and plural votes (up to a maximum of six votes for highly rated properties). A minority of about 3000 parishes adopted these arrangements and they tended to become combinations of tradesmen bound together by local interests.[3]

The Hobhouse Act 1831 introduced another sweeping change whereby every ratepayer, male or female, secured a single parochial vote. It also provided for annual elections and vote by ballot, but restricted the choice of electors to people with such a high rating qualification that most were excluded. It was however an adoptive Act and relatively few parishes operated it.

Counties

The duties of Justices of the Peace increased extensively although there were only 5000 in 1832 compared with 3000 in 1689, and the Justices struggled under the load of numerous statutes. In rural areas many Justices performed their duties conscientiously although sometimes inadequately. Justices in the towns on the other hand were all too frequently corrupt or relied implicitly upon their clerks, whose main concern was often to obtain maximum fees.

Boroughs

About 200 municipal corporations were exempt from county government under the jurisdiction of Justices of the Peace. They tended to safeguard the interests of traders and craftsmen and usually failed to provide sound administration. They were too concerned with the management of their own properties and election of members of parliament, and were largely unresponsive to local needs.

Ad Hoc Authorities

The inadequacies of the traditional local government system had resulted in the setting up of various *ad hoc* authorities as described earlier. About 200 local Acts had been passed to establish incorporated guardians of the poor, while over 1100 turnpike trusts had been formed of which the more important ones appointed permanent salaried officers and experimented with different road profiles and surfaces. Improvement commissioners were extending their activities from roads, street-lighting and police to water and gas supplies and provision of fire engines. Although the enthusiasm of some of the new authorities diminished and they were not all incorruptible, nevertheless they provided services which the traditional authorities could not supply and were in fact the beginnings of modern local government at a time when the county and borough systems were becoming increasingly ineffective.

Early Reform of Local Government

The nineteenth century saw dramatic changes in the structure of local government in England, influenced by a combination of political, social and economic changes. The concentrated new urban developments of the Industrial Revolution created an urgent need for improved public services of all kinds. This was accompanied by an increasing demand for freely elected bodies to administer local services. The pressure for reform gathered momentum in the latter part of the century backed by workers' organisations and a more enlightened social conscience aided by increased national wealth.

The Reform Act 1832 extended the vote to the middle classes and this resulted in a Liberal Government dedicated to further reform. The first statute affecting local government was the Poor Law Amendment Act 1834, which established very strong central control through the Poor Law Commissioners. Some 700 unions (groupings of parishes) replaced the 15 000 parishes for the administration of poor relief, based on convenient administrative areas, under elected Boards of Guardians of the Poor, who appointed paid officials.

The Municipal Corporations Act 1835 established the foundation of present-day local government structure by establishing elected town councils which were not concerned with the administration of justice. There were however serious limitations as a large proportion of the inhabitants could not vote and the powers of the new councils were confined to the management of corporate property, control of police and making of bye laws, although these powers were extended by subsequent statutes. The Act was applied to 178 of the 246 boroughs (London and 67 very small boroughs being excluded).

Richards[1] has described the remarkable difference of approach between the last two Acts. Poor Law reform was based on strong central control, uniform arrangements, rationalisation of areas and the ad hoc principle. The Municipal Corporations Act gave authority to local representatives subject to a minimum of central direction, maintained existing areas and created organisations which could each administer a wide range of services.

The next service demanding attention was public health. By the middle of the century about half the population lived in towns and by 1880 the proportion had increased to over two-thirds.[3] Of 50 large towns in England and Wales in 1845, scarcely one had a good drainage system and only six a really pure water supply. Living conditions were filthy and squalid, with a consequent danger of cholera and the plague.[5] Chadwick, secretary of the Poor Law Commissioners, recognised the need to improve the condition of the poor, thereby reducing the causes of ill health and the cost of poor relief.

The Public Health Act 1848 authorised the establishment of a General Board of Health overseeing local boards of health, charged with the duty of providing water supply and drainage either where the inhabitants requested it or where the death rate exceeded 23 per 1000. Municipal corporations assumed these responsibilities for their areas. The General Board of Health was abolished in 1858 but the 670 established local boards of health remained.

By the middle of the century the turnpike trusts were encountering problems with road maintenance. It had become evident that a parish was too small an area for road maintenance and in 1862 the county justices were given powers to create unions of parishes as highway districts. These proved unpopular and many villages opted out of highway districts by adopting the Public Health Act 1848 and the Local Government Act 1858, and forming their own local board of health, which entitled them to separate highway powers. The Local Government Act 1863 blocked this loophole by stipulating that only parishes with a population of at least 3000 could apply for local board of health status. However, many villages obtained this status by 1863 and some remained as urban districts for over a century until 1974. Some of the highway districts were never established and others ceased to function, resulting in responsibility for roads reverting to the parishes.[1]

The urban working class obtained the vote in 1867 but it was not until 1884 that this was extended to rural workers. A more enlightened Parliament recognised the confusion, variation and overlap of local government bodies and functions. This was particularly evident in the field of public health, where powers were vested in the vestry, guardians of the poor, local boards of health, borough councils and improvement commissioners. The Local Government Board was established in 1871 with poor law, public health and registration of births and deaths functions.

The first compulsory Public Health Act in 1875 revised and rationalised public health law and introduced a simplified pattern of urban and rural sanitary authorities, although the general structure of local government administration was still confusing and cumbersome. For instance, the urban sanitary authorities were highway authorities but not poor law authorities, while in rural areas the poor law authorities had sanitary functions and often highway responsibilities.

In 1870 the parish was given the responsibility for providing a school where it had not already been provided by a church or other voluntary agency. School attendance was made compulsory in 1876 and available free of charge in 1891.[1]

Meanwhile London had been excluded from the operation of

the Municipal Corporations Act 1835 and was probably the worst governed area in the country. The capital had expanded substantially outside the one square mile (2.6 square kilometres) occupied by the City of London, and the Corporation showed little interest in the adjoining areas. Many important services were administered by the Metropolitan Board of Works established in 1855, based on a system of indirect election through district boards. The Metropolitan Board acquired further wide-ranging powers over time, some of which it is claimed were administered corruptly.

Later Developments (1880–1944)

The Need for Reform

In the 1880s there existed a chaotic arrangement of overlapping authorities and areas. Rathbone and Pell[6] described the position in 1885 as 'a chaos of areas, a chaos of franchises, a chaos of authorities, and a chaos of rates'. The range of sizes of borough was enormous – from half a million population in Liverpool to a few hundred in Shaftesbury.[3] There could be as many as 18 different kinds of rates and even elections were held at different times, in different ways and on different franchises. It became evident that the creation of numerous *ad hoc* authorities was not conducive to maximum efficiency and that a simple system of general local authorities offered distinct advantages.[2]

Establishment of County Councils

The Local Government Act 1888 set up the county councils, with a similar framework to the boroughs, consisting of councillors elected by the ratepayers and aldermen elected by the councillors. At long last the administrative powers of Justices of the Peace outside towns were transferred to elected county councils, to the displeasure of most landowners and industrialists, although police were controlled by joint committees made up of county councillors and justices.

Initially the powers given to the counties were limited – responsibility for county roads and bridges, issue of licences, making of bye-laws and shared control of the police. In subsequent decades many other responsibilities were added.

The Act created a new administrative county for London embracing parts of Middlesex, Surrey and Kent adjoining the city of London with an area of 117 square miles (303 square kilometres). The new London County Council replaced the Metropolitan Board of Works with a structure similar to the provincial county councils and its members were elected by the ratepayers of London. The administrative area which was coincident with that of the Metropolitan Board of Works was soon to prove inadequate with the continued extensive suburban growth.

The remainder of the counties followed the geographical boundaries and no attempt was made to ensure that they embraced an adequate area or rateable value for effective operation, although some of the counties were divided for administrative convenience. Hence 62 county councils were established out of 52 geographical counties by the trisection of Yorkshire and Lincolnshire, the division of Cambridgeshire, Northamptonshire, Hampshire (1890), Suffolk and Sussex, and the creation of the new county of London. There was an enormous variation in the size and population of counties with an average population of about 500 000 and ranging from nearly $3\frac{1}{2}$ million in Lancashire to just over 20 000 in Rutland.

During the passage of the Bill representatives of the boroughs fought hard for their independence and succeeded in securing a reduction from 150 000 to 50 000 population for towns to be excluded from the counties and given county borough status. Thus 57 municipal boroughs with a population exceeding 50 000 and four other smaller boroughs – Canterbury, Chester, Worcester and Burton upon Trent – became all-purpose county boroughs with all the powers of a borough and, in addition, the powers of a county council for their area.

Thornhill[7] has described how this produced unsatisfactory one-sided changes which were difficult to reverse. Boroughs obtaining a population of 50 000 applied immediately for county borough status at the expense of administrative counties. The misgivings expressed by counties at this trend resulted in the population qualification for county borough status being increased to 75 000 in 1926. The counties argued that the county borough ratepayers made no contribution to the cost of services that they used outside borough boundaries, particularly highways. In their turn the boroughs claimed that many residents from outside their areas worked in the boroughs or used borough services without making an adequate contribution towards their cost, and they generally expressed dissatisfaction with the cost and quality of the services which the counties provided in their areas, and the extent of representation of boroughs on county councils. The financial viability of a small county could be seriously affected by the exclusion of a single county borough.

The Act of 1888 was a major step towards the concept of sub-legislatures and provision was incorporated for decentralisation from Parliament to county but this was never implemented. The Act also attempted to establish basic principles for providing monetary aid to local authorities, by isolating central aid to local government from other forms of national expenditure and thereby restricting central supervision of local administration. The majority of specific grants were replaced by a single combined grant to be paid from a separate local taxation account, funded from 40 per cent of the product of certain national taxes (assigned revenues). The system was later discontinued as the assigned revenues did not increase at the same rate as local authority expenditure and successive governments were not prepared to increase the range or proportion of revenues paid to the local taxation account. This was the beginning of a continuing controversy on the relative desirability of general grants as opposed to grants for specific purposes.[1]

Rationalisation of other Levels of Local Government

The Local Government Act 1894 converted the urban and rural sanitary districts into urban and rural district councils, in which form they remained until 1974. In urban districts the areas were the same as the former districts but the councillors were now elected by the ratepayers. Rural districts required reshaping and they acquired the duties of the rural sanitary districts and highway responsibilities of the parishes or highway districts, where established. The rural district councillors also served as members of boards of guardians.

The parishes were overhauled in an attempt to revive local life in rural areas, although many of their powers had been transferred to larger authorities. The 1894 Act established the parish council and the parish meeting for rural parishes. Every parish within a rural district was to have a parish council if its population exceeded 300; those with populations between 100 and 300 needed county council approval. Rural parishes without councils were to hold parish meetings.

Hence a dual system of local government had become established with all-purpose authorities in the larger towns (county boroughs) and a two- or three-tier system elsewhere with powers shared between the county councils and district councils. In rural areas the introduction of parish councils and meetings produced a three-tier system, with three levels of local government. In practice the county councils had little control over district councils with their variety of functions and the two tiers tended to operate as separate units, which was not conducive to the most effective development of services.[7]

The Local Government Act 1899 overhauled local government

administration in London by replacing numerous district boards and vestries by 28 metropolitan borough councils. It was believed that the boroughs would act as a counterweight to the London County Council as they were given responsibility for public health, housing, rating, libraries and recreational services. It was not foreseen at that time that most new duties would be assigned to the county council, thus accentuating the imbalance.[1] The Corporation of the City of London remained a separate independent administrative unit.

The pattern of local government structure thus established was to remain for over half a century – until 1963 in London and 1974 in the remainder of England and Wales, and this is illustrated in Figure 1.

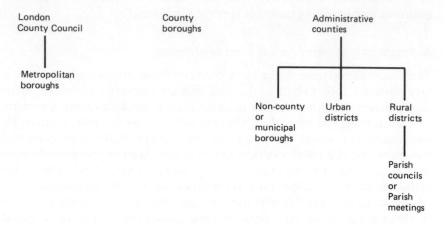

FIGURE 1   *Local government structure – England and Wales, 1899–1974*
(London, 1899–1963)

Growth of Population, Towns and Transport

The population of England and Wales was increasing at a considerable rate, rising from 26 million in 1881 to 38 million in 1921 – an increase of 46 per cent in 40 years. This increase was not distributed evenly throughout the country and was concentrated primarily in the towns which extended into the surrounding countryside. These developments undermined local authority boundaries and caused conflict between urban and rural authorities, as the majority of rural district councils and county councils were opposed to town boundary extensions and the conferment of county borough status. Between 1889 and 1925 there were 109 extensions of county borough areas and an increase in the number of county boroughs from 61 to 82, involving a combined loss to the counties of 350 000 acres (140 000 hectares), 3 million population and about £14½ million in rateable value. An Act of 1926 increased the minimum qualifying population for county borough status to 75 000 and made the procedure more difficult by replacing the provisional order by private Act. In consequence no new county boroughs were established between 1927 and 1964.

Changes in the mode and speed of transport must be a major factor in determining the extent of administrative areas for purposes of local government. The parish could be traversed during the day on foot, while the county could be covered by a man on horseback between sunrise and sunset.[8] Increased mobility was given by the railways and the later invention of the internal combustion engine extended the range of people's mobility and created an urgent need for better highways.

Local Government Act 1929

The 1929 Act contained a number of important provisions, of which one was the abolition of the only remaining *ad hoc* authority – the Guardians of the Poor. Their functions (poor law, registration and hospital service) were transferred to the county councils and county borough councils. Another aim was to improve the condition of roads in country areas to keep pace with the increasing number of vehicles by transferring the highway powers of rural districts to the county councils. Towns with a population exceeding 20 000 could claim highway powers over county roads within their boundaries and all urban authorities retained responsibility for minor or unclassified roads. Rural districts and towns with less than 20 000 population could be given delegated powers over county roads in their areas but this did not operate very satisfactorily and diminished over time. There is a strong case for confining highway activities to the larger authorities with the necessary technical expertise and resources.[1]

The Act also recognised the need for regional planning over wider areas than those of individual local authority units. It empowered county councils to act jointly with other authorities in the preparation or adoption of town planning schemes.

On central government financial assistance the Act made provision for a general exchequer contribution replacing assigned revenues and based on a formula weighted to favour those authorities with greater demands or smaller resources than average. Increased grants were needed to offset the loss in rates resulting from the derating of agricultural and industrial properties.

Finally, to encourage rationalisation of local government administration, the 1929 Act required the county councils to make a decennial review of their district councils. As a result of these county reviews the numbers of urban and rural districts were each reduced by about 25 per cent.

The Local Government Act 1933 aimed at producing a uniform constitutional code and a framework of general powers for local authorities outside London.[2] Similar arrangements were introduced for London in 1939. After 1901 the population of the county of London declined while that of surrounding areas increased and there was considerable support for the view that many activities such as public health, housing, town planning and transport could be administered effectively only by a single authority controlling a larger area than the administrative county. In the event the London Passenger Transport Board was formed in 1933 and took over London's public transport services.

Loss of Functions to Central Government

The twentieth century saw a steady transfer of functions from local to central government. In 1930 the licensing of passenger road services was transferred from local authorities to area traffic commissioners and this was followed in 1936 by the transfer of 3500 miles (5630 kilometres) of trunk roads to the Ministry of Transport.

The Unemployment Act 1934 transferred to the Assistance Board responsibility for able-bodied unemployed who had exhausted their rights to unemployment insurance benefit. The supplementation of old age and widows' pensions followed in 1940. The National Health Service Act 1946 transferred hospital administration to regional hospital boards – a revival of *ad hoc* authorities – while other Acts pruned still further local authority welfare services.

Local authority public utility services were drastically reduced by the nationalisation of gas and electricity supplies, and almost half of the airports owned by local authorities were transferred to the Ministry of Aviation.[8]

Increased Central Government Control

A steady increase of control by central government of local government activities occurred in the twentieth century. This development stemmed from a fear that local authorities might become too ambitious in response to popular demands. Later, grants in aid were coupled with a checking mechanism to ensure that money given to local authorities was spent economically and effectively. Thus the block grant introduced in 1929 was accompanied by a provision which gave the Minister of Health power to reduce the grant if he considered that the expenditure of the council had not been effective. Later legislation contained even more positive direction and control. For instance, in the field of education, the 1921 Act required local authorities to submit schemes for approval, while the 1944 Act required the Minister of Education, *inter alia*, 'to secure the effective execution by local authorities under his control and direction of the national policy for providing a varied and comprehensive educational service in every area'. Hence the present century has seen a significant growth in the scale of services provided by local authorities, despite the loss of some functions to central government, accompanied by an increase in supervision and control by central government departments over local administration and an increase in aid from the national Exchequer.[1] One effective controlling device is the district audit described in Chapter 9.

Main Local Authority Functions

The position with regard to the main local authority functions in the first half of the twentieth century is now briefly examined to elucidate the overall picture.

Education

In 1900 the school-leaving age was raised from 12 to 14. The Education Act 1902 abolished the 2500 school boards and transferred their functions to 328 local authorities. The allocation of responsibilities was rather fragmented, with county councils and county borough councils empowered to provide both elementary and secondary education, but in addition non-county boroughs with at least 10 000 population and urban districts with a minimum population of 20 000 at the 1901 census were responsible for elementary education. By the 1930s many boroughs and urban districts had grown extensively and had no educational powers although they were larger than some educational authorities.

Later Acts introduced the provision of meals for children in elementary schools, medical inspection and treatment, and nursery and continuation schools. The Education Act 1944 concentrated educational administration in the counties and county boroughs, although limited powers could be delegated to towns with populations over 60 000. The Act introduced the principle of secondary education for all and a new classification of schools. Part-time, further and technical education, free medical treatment and school meals services were all extended and secondary education fees abolished. The school-leaving age was eventually raised to 16 and local education authorities co-operated in the provision of advanced courses to avoid duplication. Later, the 1962 Act compelled local authorities to award grants to students on the higher-level courses (two 'A' level entry).

Highways

The last turnpike trust was dissolved in 1895 and the following year the requirement for a steam traction engine to be preceded by a man carrying a red flag was repealed and the speed restriction increased from 4 to 12 miles per hour ($6\frac{1}{2}$ to 19 kilometres per hour), thereby giving an impetus to motor car production.[9] A national road improvement grant was created in 1909 to provide funds for the development and improvement of roads. The national significance of roads was further recognised by the establishment of the Ministry of Transport in 1919, and in the following year a national road fund was set up from a tax on motor vehicles to assist local authorities with road improvements. The Local Government Act 1929 reduced the number of highway authorities in Great Britain from 2210 to 1415, and Acts of 1936 and 1946 created trunk roads, which were the responsibility of the Ministry of Transport.

By 1933 the number of vehicles annually licensed in Great Britain exceeded 2 million, the total mileage of roads exceeded 176 000 and the annual cost of maintenance and reasonable improvement was £45 million, engaging the services of 3000 engineers. The need for road safety measures had become apparent as, in 1937, 6600 people were killed on the roads and 226 402 injured.[9] There was also an indisputable need for a network of arterial roads or motorways and by-pass roads around numerous large towns to cope with the increasing number of vehicles and heavier loads.

Public Health, Housing and Town Planning

Until the latter part of the nineteenth century public health activities were mainly confined to water supply, drainage, sewerage and the abatement of nuisances, because of the lack of knowledge of bacteriology. In the present century vast strides have been made in the provision of personal as well as environmental health services. The average annual death rate in Great Britain fell from 20.3 per 1000 in 1871–80 to 10.6 per 1000 in 1921–30. The expectation of life at birth has nearly doubled in the last century. These improvements stem from advances in science and medicine, the development of environmental services, and the introduction of town and country planning and personal medical services, coupled with unemployment benefits, pensions and a much improved standard of living.[3]

Some council houses and flats were built in the nineteenth century to replace slums, but it was not until after the First World War that the provision of public housing was recognised as a social need. Acts passed during 1919–25 empowered borough and urban and rural district councils to build houses for the working classes and provided financial assistance. Much later, the Housing Act 1949 extended public housing provision to cover all members of the community and introduced grants for the improvement of older properties.

The earliest town and country planning legislation empowered borough and district councils to prepare planning schemes for their areas, but because of the complex procedures and the liability for payment of compensation, relatively little of the country was subject to operative planning schemes in 1939. During the Second World War three substantial reports were prepared on industrial location, compensation and betterment and the countryside which laid the foundations for post-war legislation. Wartime Acts resulted in the whole country being subject to interim development control and gave local authorities the power to deal with 'blitzed' and 'blighted' areas.

The Town and Country Planning Act 1947 replaced planning schemes with positive development plans and county councils and county borough councils became the local planning authorities. The Act also contained provisions for the payment of development charges on permitted development and compensation from a £300 million fund for the acquisition of the unrealised development potential of all land in Great Britain. The latter provisions were repealed in 1953. Later Acts modified planning law with the introduction of more realistic structure and local plans and changes with regard to land acquisition and financial aspects.

Police

Increased central control of police forces was introduced in 1919, when the Home Secretary was empowered to make regulations applying to all police forces. A Police Council was also established, made up of police officers and providing a channel for consultation by the Home Secretary. At that time there were 48 police forces with less than 25 men, which could not conceivably provide maximum efficiency, yet municipal borough police forces were not amalgamated with county forces until 1948.

Municipal Trading and Other Services

The earliest activity was the charging of fees or tolls for markets and fairs.[7] The latter part of the nineteenth century and the first half of the twentieth century saw the development of many municipal enterprises including water supply, gas supply, electricity supply, tramways and, later, omnibuses, markets, crematoria, slaughter houses, airports and racecourses. Various Acts have empowered local authorities to provide libraries, museums and art galleries and other forms of cultural, entertainment and recreational facilities. Electricity undertakings were nationalised in 1947 and gas undertakings in 1948.

Conclusions

The nature and extent of the changes in local conditions and needs over the period under consideration show the advisability of periodic reviews of local government structure and services. There is an increasing and rather unfortunate tendency to transfer locally administered services to central government and new *ad hoc* authorities. County councils and county borough councils have been strengthened at the expense of municipal borough and district councils, to ensure adequate resources and a uniform approach and standard of service over a larger area.

References

1. RICHARDS, P. G., *The Reformed Local Government System* (Allen and Unwin, 1975).
2. HART, W. O. and GARNER, J. F., *Hart's Introduction to the Law of Local Government and Administration* (Butterworth, 1973).
3. SMELLIE, K. B., *A History of Local Government* (Allen and Unwin, 1969).
4. WEBB, S. and B., *English Local Government, the Parish and the County*, vol. 1 (Longman, 1929).
5. CHADWICK, E., *Report on the Sanitary Condition of the Labouring Population* (H.M.S.O., 1842) and *Report on the State of Large Towns* (H.M.S.O., 1845).
6. RATHBONE, W. and PELL, W., *Local Government and Taxation* (Sonnenschein, 1885).
7. THORNHILL, W., *The Growth and Reform of English Local Government* (Weidenfeld and Nicolson, 1971).

8. ROBSON, W. A., *The Development of Local Government* (Allen and Unwin, 1954).
9. SCOTT-GILES, C. W., *The Road Goes On* (Epworth Press, 1946).

CHAPTER TWO

WINDS OF CHANGE

Need for Reform

By the middle of the twentieth century many recognised the need for reform of the local government structure to deal effectively with the continually changing conditions resulting in more complex administrative problems. The structure was still based essentially on the Acts of 1888 and 1894, whose main provisions were described in Chapter 1. Admittedly the period between 1888 and 1926 had seen the creation of 21 new county boroughs and extensions to many others, and this had resulted in a substantial loss of funds to county councils. Some rationalisation of district council areas had occurred through county reviews under the Local Government Act 1929.

The earlier *ad hoc* authorities dealing with local government functions had been rescinded but new ones were being created in the 1940s. Local authorities had been allocated many new activities, particularly in the field of personal welfare. One major deficiency in the structure was the clear distinction made between urban and rural authorities, based to some extent on the doubtful premise that a lower range and level of services were acceptable in rural areas. In practice the two types of area were very much interdependent and this called for concerted approach and action. A structure suited to Victorian conditions was not necessarily the best arrangement for the middle of the twentieth century because of large changes in population distribution, including the rapid growth of the conurbations, improved transport facilities and the development and widespread use of motor vehicles, technological developments generally and the demand for more and improved services.

It was questionable whether small towns, despite their long histories and traditions, were still suited to be the nuclei of local government administrative areas, largely because of inadequate resources. The variations in size, area and functions of local authorities were enormous, with the largest English county having a population eighty times greater than the smallest and a host of very small county districts surpassed in population by many parishes.

Some services such as planning and major highways required administering over large areas, certainly not less than counties, yet the urban authorities understandably were reluctant to lose services to the county councils, whom many of them believed to be already too powerful. It was evident that different services possessed different functional criteria and that groups of interdependent services required separate examination when determining the types of authority to which they should be allocated. Meanwhile, some interesting developments occurred in the provision of new and expanding towns.

Hence the period 1945–70 saw the setting up of a number of Royal Commissions and the publication of several White Papers concerned with local government reorganisation. The remainder of this chapter is devoted to a broad consideration of these events culminating in the 1971 White Paper and the Local Government Act 1972, which are both dealt with in Chapter 3.

Immediate Post-war Developments

1945 White Paper on Local Government

The Coalition Government published a White Paper in 1945[1] which stated that reports from local authority associations had shown there to be 'no general desire to disrupt the existing structure of local government or to abandon in favour of some form of regional government the main features of the county and county borough system'. The Government however believed that there was need and scope for improvements within the general framework. It accordingly proposed the establishment of a Boundary Commission to examine and, if necessary, alter the boundaries of county, county borough and county district councils, subject to certain provisos.

As Robson[2] has described, it was a misleading document as the local authority associations approached all had sectional interests and some unbiased evidence could have been more useful. The White Paper assumed that the existing local government structure was sound and effective although there was substantial evidence to the contrary.

Local Government Boundary Commission

The Local Government (Boundary Commission) Act 1945 established a Boundary Commission authorised to make boundary changes outside London but it was given no power over functions and could not introduce any new type of authority. Hence any form of regional government was eliminated from the outset.

The Commission commenced work with some high ideals – 'our

task is to make, so far as is practicable, all local government authorities, both individually and collectively, effective and convenient units'.[3] It then proceeded to examine the problem for two years and reported that it was nonsense to consider boundaries without functions.[4] The Commission highlighted the problems of disparity in size and resources between different authorities, lack of cohesion of administrative units in conurbations, increased central control of local government, haphazard allocation of functions to authorities and conflicts over boundaries between counties and county boroughs.

The Commission recommended a new structure whereby seventeen of the largest cities with a minimum population of 200 000 would be retained as one-tier authorities under the title one-tier counties. The remainder of England and Wales was to be administered on a two-tier system with a minimum county population of 200 000 subdivided into boroughs and urban and rural districts. A new type of authority termed county boroughs with populations in the range 60 000 to 200 000 would have all functions except planning, main roads, police and fire service. These proposals proved unacceptable and the Commission was dissolved in 1949.

Nevertheless, the need for reform remained. Consultations continued between the local authority associations and the Government, against a background of the transfer of functions from local government to new independent authorities (hospitals, and gas and electricity undertakings) or central government departments (valuations for rating). The consultations culminated in the issue of another White Paper,[5] which again supported the retention of the broad framework of local government subject to such overhaul and improvements as were needed to bring it up to date.

The Local Government Act 1958 and Consequent Developments

The Local Government Act 1958 established two Local Government Commissions, one for England and one for Wales. The Commissions were required to review the areas of groups of counties and county boroughs outside Greater London defined as 'general review areas' and in addition the English Commission was to make separate reviews of the five conurbations defined as 'special review areas', namely Tyneside, West Yorkshire, South East Lancashire, Merseyside and the West Midlands.

In the general review areas the Commissions had wide powers to obtain information, hold local inquiries and to make proposals for the abolition, amalgamation or alteration of existing counties and county boroughs and for the establishment of new ones, with the proviso that any new county borough should have a minimum population of 100 000. The English Commission's powers in the special review areas were extended to cover non-county boroughs and county districts, including their functions. The Commissions were to forward their findings to the Minister, who was empowered to embody them in proposals for approval by both Houses of Parliament.

Following the general reviews, county councils were required to review the boundaries of county districts and they were empowered to recommend the reduction in status of small non-county boroughs to rural boroughs. Rural boroughs would form part of rural districts and so would have much reduced powers being more akin to rural parishes, although they could retain the charter and mayor but no aldermen.

The Commissions carried out their investigations continuously from 1958 to 1966. The procedure established in the Act proved very cumbersome with ample opportunity for public participation at every stage and Richards[6] describes the tendency for each consultative stage to reduce the amount of recommended change. Furthermore, the Commissions often seemed to become entangled with minor issues, while on matters of major significance they received little support from the Government.

The English Commission made many recommendations, some of which were approved, but did not complete its investigations before it voluntarily suspended its activities in 1966. The principal approved recommendations included the amalgamation of one small county, the Soke of Peterborough, with Huntingdonshire, and another, the Isle of Ely, with Cambridgeshire. Other approved proposals included the creation of the new county boroughs of Dudley, Solihull, Warley (Smethwick), West Bromwich, Walsall, Wolverhampton, Luton, Torbay, Teesside and Hartlepools. The boundaries of many boroughs were extended.

However, the proposal to amalgamate Rutland with Leicestershire was not ratified after four years of spirited resistance by this very small county, despite its evident lack of resources.

The Welsh Commission recommended that the thirteen administrative counties, including Monmouthshire, be reduced by amalgamations to five, but subsequently amended to seven. These proposals were rejected by the Minister. A White Paper issued in 1967 proposed five counties (later increased to six), three county boroughs and 36 districts (later reduced to 35) in place of the existing 164 county districts.

In 1966 the Government decided that the patchwork approach of the English Commission was unsatisfactory and its terms of reference prevented it from securing effective reorganisation of the structure for the whole country. Hence the Local Government Commissions were dissolved in 1967 and county reviews discontinued but without prejudice to undecided proposals in both cases.

At the same time as these developments were taking place proposals for the restructuring of local government in London were being formulated and implemented, and these are considered later in the chapter. Another interesting development was the establishment of two committees by the Minister in 1964, at the request of the four principal local authority associations, because of evident concern at the low quality of some of the officers and members joining local government. The Maud Committee's terms of reference were 'to consider in the light of modern conditions how local government might best continue to attract and retain people (both elected representatives and principal officers) of the calibre necessary to ensure its maximum effectiveness',[7] while those of the Mallaby Committee were 'to consider the existing methods of recruiting local government officers and of using them; and what changes might help local authorities to get the best possible service and help their officers to give it'.[8]

Both Committees were concerned essentially with recruitment but, in their reports published in 1967, both expressed concern at deteriorating conditions, an excess of central control and the need for changed attitudes by all concerned with local government. They found that resources were not adequate to meet the ever increasing demands placed upon them.

The Mallaby Report[8] made some important recommendations with regard to recruitment, career prospects, selection procedure, training at various levels, use of staff, internal organisation, mobility of staff and action by professional associations, central government departments and local authority associations. The more important staffing recommendations are considered in Chapter 6.

The Maud Report[7] considered that the country was not getting full value in terms of human happiness for the time spent and for the increasing capital expenditure standing in 1967 at £3000 million per annum (9 per cent of the gross national product). These deficiencies stemmed from the local government structure of areas, authorities and functions but also from over-involvement by elected members in the work of authorities, an excessive number of committees and sub-committees, too much fragmentation of work between separate departments, lack of calibre of some elected members and officers entering the local government service and other internal organisational matters. The report contains excellent recommendations for the reform of internal organisation, relations between central and local government and between local authorities and the public. These aspects will be considered in some detail in later chapters.

Royal Commission on Local Government in England, 1966–9

Procedure

A Royal Commission under Lord Redcliffe-Maud was established in 1966[9] 'to consider the structure of local government in England, outside Greater London, in relation to its existing functions; and to make recommendations for authorities and boundaries, and for functions and their division, having regard to the size and character of the areas in which these can be most effectively exercised and the need to sustain a viable system of democracy'.

Evidence was obtained from a total of 2156 witnesses, which included a large number of individual local authorities, and many professional bodies and private persons. Oral evidence was taken in public from government departments, local authority associations, the Association of Education Committees and the National and Local Government Officers' Association (NALGO). Witnesses favoured a variety of proposals: some favoured regional councils backed by second-tier authorities for local matters; others favoured the city region concept, possibly as a single-tier system; others preferring an upper tier with great operational and executive powers and little responsibility to second-tier authorities were offset by those who wanted the top tier to be limited to a few functions and the majority of services to be provided at local level. The wide variation in views served to illustrate the complexity of the problem and the strength of sectional interests.

Existing Deficiencies

The Commission was unanimous in the view that 'local government in England needed a new structure and a new map'. It was 'in a sense a random growth' which had 'not been planned systematically in the light of what it has to do and the social and geographical conditions of each place'. The Commission identified the following four basic defects in the structure existing at that time.

1. Local government areas did not fit the pattern of life and work in modern England.
2. The fragmentation of England into 79 county boroughs and 45 counties, exercising independent jurisdictions and dividing town from country, made proper planning of development and

transport impossible. This has often led to an atmosphere of hostility between county boroughs and counties and made it harder to decide difficult questions on their merits.

3. The division of responsibility within each county between the county council and a number of county district councils, together with the position of county boroughs as islands in the counties, meant that services which should have been in the hands of one authority were fragmented among several, thus making it more difficult to meet comprehensively the needs of individuals.

4. Many local authorities were too small, in size and revenue, and in consequence too short of highly qualified manpower and technical equipment, to be able to do their work as well as it could and should have been done.

General Principles Formulated by Commission

The Commission felt that these structural and other defects posed a fundamental question – what size of authority, or range of sizes, in terms of population and of area, is needed for the democratic and efficient provision of particular services and for local self-government as a whole? After considering each of the main services the Commission decided that the answers to that question must be found by seeking to apply to each part of the country the following general principles.

1. Local authority areas must be so defined that they enable citizens and their elected representatives to have a sense of common purpose.

2. The areas must be based upon the interdependence of town and country.

3. In each part of the country all services concerned with the physical environment (planning, transport and major development) must be in the hands of one authority, with areas large enough to enable these authorities to meet the pressing land needs of the growing population.

4. All personal services (education, personal social services, health and housing), being closely linked in operation and effect, must also be in the hands of one authority.

5. If possible, both the 'environmental' and the 'personal' groups of services should be in the hands of the same authority, because the influence of the one on the other is great and likely to increase. Concentrating responsibility for all main local government services in a single authority for each area, as in county boroughs, helps to make the idea of local self-government a reality. Through allocation of priorities and co-ordinated

use of resources, a single authority can relate its programmes for all services to objectives for its area considered as a whole.

6. Authorities must, however, be larger than most county boroughs and all county districts if they are to command the resources and skilled manpower which are needed to provide services with maximum efficiency.

7. The size of authorities must vary over a wide range if areas are to match the pattern of population, but a minimum population is necessary. The Commission suggested a minimum of around 250 000.

8. At the other end of the scale, authorities must not be so large in terms of population that organisation of their business becomes difficult and the elected representatives cannot keep in touch with the people affected by their policies. This is especially important with personal services, where the Commission concluded that a population of not much more than 1 million should be the maximum.

9. Where the area required for planning and other environmental services contains too large a population for the personal services, a single authority for all services would not be appropriate; and in these parts of the country, responsibilities must be clearly divided between two levels and related services kept together.

10. The new local government pattern should so far as is practicable stem from the existing one. Wherever the case for change is in doubt, the common interests, traditions and loyalties inherent in the present pattern, and the strength of existing services as going concerns, should be respected.

Commission's Approach

The Commission first concentrated on the 'city region' concept, as it had the strong support of the Ministry of Housing and Local Government. This concept highlighted the increasing mobility of people but opinions of witnesses differed as to the number of city regions needed for the country as a whole (between 25 and 45). Many witnesses suggested that second-tier authorities would also be required to ensure effective contact between elected representatives and the people, but this would have resulted in many very small authorities with inadequate resources and the splitting of personal services. Furthermore, city regions were not practicable in some parts of the country.

The Commission then examined other alternatives. For instance, the country could be divided into between 130 and 140 areas with some coherence stemming from internal social and economic ties but they would be too small to employ the staff needed for the efficient provision of any of the main services.

The Commission was influenced strongly by those who advocated the need for representation at grass-roots level and saw the need for local councils, not to provide main services, but to promote and watch over the particular interests of communities in cities, towns and villages throughout England. They also saw a place for new representative institutions with authority over areas larger than city regions and not dissimilar to the regional economic planning councils, which would handle the broader planning issues and work out economic strategy in collaboration with central government. Finally, there was the need for authorities in between the previous two levels, with operational responsibility for all local government services, where they would form coherent units for carrying out environmental services, have populations between 250 000 and 1 million for the efficient performance of personal services and could be looked after effectively and democratically by a single council. If these conditions could not be met responsibility would need to be divided between authorities at two tiers.

Commission's Proposals

The Commission proposed that the greater part of England should be divided into 58 unitary authorities, embracing both town and country, responsible for all services. Major towns which provided a focal point for the commerce and cultural life of the surrounding area would also be the centre for local government. The populations of the areas administered by the unitary authorities would vary from 195 000 to over 1 million.

The remainder of the country, excluding London, was shown divided into three metropolitan areas around Birmingham, Liverpool and Manchester. In these areas responsibility for services would be divided between a metropolitan authority, whose key functions would be planning, transport and major development, and 20 metropolitan district authorities, whose key functions would be education, personal social services, health and housing.

The Commission further proposed that these 61 new local government areas should be grouped, together with Greater London, in eight provinces, each with its own provincial council. Provincial councils would be elected by the authorities for the unitary and metropolitan areas and Greater London, but would also include co-opted members. The key function of these councils would be to settle the provincial strategy and planning framework within which the main authorities would operate, thus replacing the regional economic planning councils, and to collaborate with central government in the economic and social development of each province.

Throughout the 61 areas, local councils initially representing the displaced boroughs, urban districts and parishes should be elected to represent and communicate the wishes of cities, towns and villages in all matters of special concern to the inhabitants. Their sole duty would be to represent local opinion, but they would have the right to be consulted on matters of special interest to local inhabitants and could play a part with services appropriate to their resources and subject to the agreement of the main authority.

One member of the Commission, Derek Senior, was so convinced that the right approach was to create city regions that he produced a memorandum of dissent in which he proposed five provincial councils, 35 city regions, 148 district councils and numerous local councils. The city regions would be directly elected and responsible for the planning, transport and development functions, capital investment programming, police, fire and education, while the directly elected district councils would have health, housing and personal services functions.

Reaction to Commission's Report

Public reaction to the unitary authority concept was in general unfavourable. Of the four principal local authority associations only one, the Association of Municipal Corporations, supported the proposals, but the others preferred a two-tier system to prevent the risk of rural interests being disregarded by dominant urban authorities. The Senior alternative proposals appeared to carry greater support. There was an evident desire for increased representation and a minimum of reform.

A Government White Paper[10] in 1970 proposed a new local government structure based on 51 unitary areas and five metropolitan areas – Merseyside (Liverpool), Selnec (Manchester), West Midlands, West Yorkshire and South Hampshire. The Commission's proposals for eight provincial councils was deferred but the establishment of local councils was accepted. Other recommendations included the abolition of the office of alderman, improvements in councillors' allowances, fewer committees, delegation of more detail to officers, review of non-financial controls and less statutory control.

The Labour Government intended to promote a Bill in the 1971–2 session of Parliament to introduce the new structure. However, in the June 1970 General Election the Conservatives gained power and they opposed the unitary concept and intended to retain a two-tier structure. The result was the publication of another White Paper[11] in 1971 containing alternative proposals which formed the basis of the Local Government Act 1972 and which are described in Chapter 3.

In 1970 the Labour Government had also proposed a new local government structure for Wales based on three unitary authorities, with the remainder of the country divided into counties and local councils. The proposals were largely opposed by the Welsh population and did not materialise because of the subsequent change of Government.

Local Government in London

The structure of local government in London as described in Chapter 1 was altered significantly by the London Government Act 1963. This Act replaced 52 Metropolitan boroughs with 32 London boroughs, having populations in the main between 200 000 and 250 000. Yet at the same time the area of the administrative county of London, to be administered by the Greater London Council, was extended to occupy the whole of the county of Middlesex and parts of the neighbouring counties of Hertfordshire, Essex, Surrey and Kent. The City of London remained independent and its Common Council has the powers of a London borough council. The twelve inner London boroughs together with the City of London contained the area of the former London County Council and educational functions in this area are administered by the Inner London Education Authority (ILEA). Figure 2 shows the arrangement and titles of the 32 London boroughs. These arrangements came into effect on 1 April 1965 and the Greater London Council (G.L.C.) administers an area of over 1610 square kilometres with a population in 1965 of about 8 million.

The Greater London Council was made responsible for main roads, traffic management, strategic planning, main drainage, fire and ambulance services, refuse disposal and building control. It shares responsibility for planning and housing with London boroughs and the City of London. The London boroughs have responsibility for personal health, welfare and children's services, libraries, cemeteries, allotments, swimming baths, refuse collection and local roads.

The new structure offered some distinct advantages, with the Greater London Council having a much larger area embracing most of the built-up area of Greater London matched with ample resources to fulfil its important functions. The enlarged London boroughs were also given substantial functions which enabled them to make

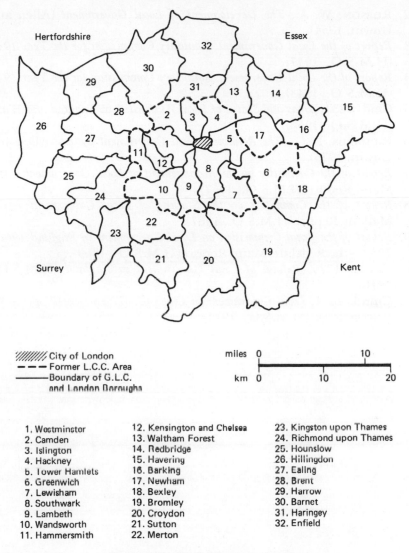

Hertfordshire

Essex

Surrey

Kent

///// City of London
— — — Former L.C.C. Area
———— Boundary of G.L.C.
and London Boroughs

miles 0   10
km 0   10   20

1. Westminster	12. Kensington and Chelsea	23. Kingston upon Thames
2. Camden	13. Waltham Forest	24. Richmond upon Thames
3. Islington	14. Redbridge	25. Hounslow
4. Hackney	15. Havering	26. Hillingdon
5. Tower Hamlets	16. Barking	27. Ealing
6. Greenwich	17. Newham	28. Brent
7. Lewisham	18. Bexley	29. Harrow
8. Southwark	19. Bromley	30. Barnet
9. Lambeth	20. Croydon	31. Haringey
10. Wandsworth	21. Sutton	32. Enfield
11. Hammersmith	22. Merton	

FIGURE 2   *Local government – London*

a worthwhile contribution in the two-tier structure. The one major deficiency has stemmed from the overlap of a few important activities, which has produced difficulties.

References

1. Cmd. 6579, *Local Government in England and Wales during the Period of Reconstruction* (H.M.S.O., 1945).

2. ROBSON, W. A., *The Development of Local Government* (Allen and Unwin, 1954).
3. *Report of the Local Government Boundary Commission for the Year 1946* (H.M.S.O., 1947).
4. *Report of the Local Government Boundary Commission for the Year 1947* (H.M.S.O., 1948).
5. Cmd. 9831, *Areas and Status of Local Authorities in England and Wales* (H.M.S.O., 1956).
6. RICHARDS, P. G., *The Reformed Local Government System* (Allen and Unwin, 1975).
7. *Report of the Committee on the Management of Local Government* – the Maud Report (H.M.S.O., 1967).
8. *Report of the Committee on the Staffing of Local Government* – the Mallaby Report (H.M.S.O., 1967).
9. *Report of the Royal Commission on Local Government in England 1966–1969* – the Redcliffe-Maud Report (H.M.S.O., 1969).
10. Cmnd. 4276, *Reform of Local Government in England* (H.M.S.O., 1970).
11. Cmnd. 4584, *Local Government in England: Government Proposals for Reorganisation* (H.M.S.O., 1971).

CHAPTER THREE

LOCAL GOVERNMENT STRUCTURE
SINCE 1974

Reorganisation Proposals

In 1971 the new Conservative Government's proposals emerged in two White Papers – one for England[1] and the other for Scotland[2] – and a consultative document – for Wales.[3]

The White Paper covering local government in England recognised the validity of the arguments for large authorities for the efficient operation of some services and for smaller authorities for grass-roots democracy. Hence the compromise solution of a two-tier structure was proposed, consisting essentially of counties and districts. Metropolitan counties were proposed in the densely populated conurbations, each divided into metropolitan districts having more powers than other districts.

A radical reorganisation of boroughs and urban and rural districts was proposed to provide larger districts which would have greater resources and thus be better fitted to undertake the responsibilities allocated to them. A Local Government Boundary Commission was to make proposals for the arrangement of districts outside the metropolitan counties and its report in 1972 proposed 278 districts with an average population of about 100 000. The place of the rural parish was also recognised but it was to have powers rather than duties.

The Welsh consultative document proposed that Wales should be reorganised into seven new counties and 36 districts. Community councils would be created at the parish level.

Local Government Act 1972

The Local Government Act 1972 gave effect to the proposals contained in the 1971 White Paper[1] and consultative document,[3] creating a new local government structure in England and Wales, with a reallocation of functions. It also contained new provisions covering the administration of local authorities including such matters as registration of electors and conduct of elections, general procedural arrangements, discharge of functions and finance. This Act largely replaced the Local Government Act 1933 and incorporated, with some modifications, the provisions of the London Government Act

1963 relating to local government in London. However, the structure of London local government was barely changed and remained as described in Chapter 2.

The new structure came into force on 1 April 1974 and comprises the following arrangements.

England and Wales are divided into counties and districts, with Monmouthshire and Newport transferred to Wales. There are 45 counties in England and eight in Wales, as shown in Figure 3, of which only five are entirely coincident with the boundaries of the former administrative counties. Six of the English counties are termed metropolitan counties, embracing the major urban conurbations of Greater Manchester, Merseyside, South Yorkshire, Tyne and Wear, West Yorkshire and West Midlands. The remaining 39 English counties are often referred to as non-metropolitan counties.

In the six metropolitan counties there are 36 metropolitan districts with similar constitutions to those of other districts but extended functions which are described later in the chapter. There are 296 non-metropolitan districts in England and 37 in Wales, some of which are wholly urban, some wholly rural and many others both urban and rural in character. This has resulted in a large reduction in the number of second-tier authorities, which previously amounted to 1333, made up of county and non-county boroughs and urban and rural districts. District councils were empowered to submit a petition to the Privy Council for borough status and many submissions have been made and approved. Procurement of borough status entitles the council to elect a mayor and deputy mayor but has little other practical significance.

At third-tier level, English rural parishes remain and new parishes may be created and existing ones abolished. Hence the pattern of parishes can change and, as the earlier distinction between urban and rural districts has been removed, there is no restriction on the districts in which parishes can be created.[4] Former rural parish councils continue and new ones were to be established in former boroughs and urban districts where the Secretary of State so directed. The population limit for new parish councils is either 150 or 200 electors, the lower limit applying where a parish meeting has requested one. In Wales, community councils supersede the former boroughs, urban districts and rural parishes.

Local Government Boundary Commissions were established on a permanent basis for England and Wales to review local government boundaries and local electoral arrangements.

The total number of principal councils (above third-tier level) in England and Wales, including London, was reduced from 1425 to 456. There was however still a great diversity of population,

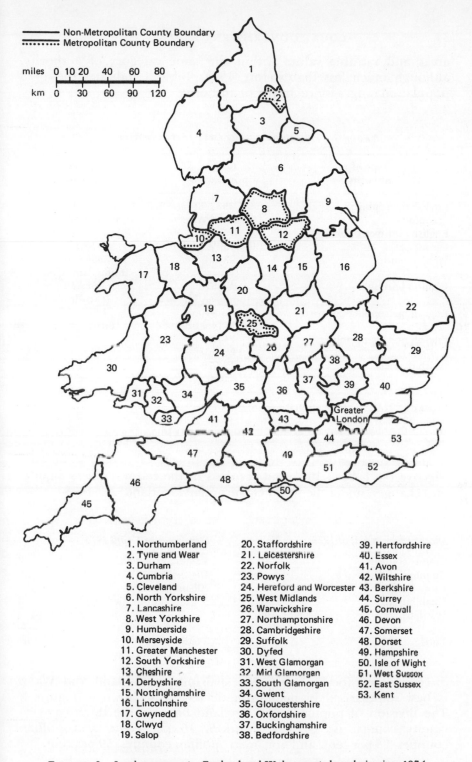

Non-Metropolitan County Boundary
Metropolitan County Boundary

miles 0 10 20 40   60   80
km 0   30   60   90   120

1
2
3
4
5
6
7
8
9
10
11
12
13
14
15
16
17
18
19
20
21
22
23
24
25
26
27
28
29
30
31
32
33
34
35
36
37
38
39
40
41
42
43
44
45
46
47
48
49
50
51
52
53
Greater London

1. Northumberland	20. Staffordshire	39. Hertfordshire
2. Tyne and Wear	21. Leicestershire	40. Essex
3. Durham	22. Norfolk	41. Avon
4. Cumbria	23. Powys	42. Wiltshire
5. Cleveland	24. Hereford and Worcester	43. Berkshire
6. North Yorkshire	25. West Midlands	44. Surrey
7. Lancashire	26. Warwickshire	45. Cornwall
8. West Yorkshire	27. Northamptonshire	46. Devon
9. Humberside	28. Cambridgeshire	47. Somerset
10. Merseyside	29. Suffolk	48. Dorset
11. Greater Manchester	30. Dyfed	49. Hampshire
12. South Yorkshire	31. West Glamorgan	50. Isle of Wight
13. Cheshire	32. Mid Glamorgan	51. West Sussex
14. Derbyshire	33. South Glamorgan	52. East Sussex
15. Nottinghamshire	34. Gwent	53. Kent
16. Lincolnshire	35. Gloucestershire	
17. Gwynedd	36. Oxfordshire	
18. Clwyd	37. Buckinghamshire	
19. Salop	38. Bedfordshire	

FIGURE 3   *Local government – England and Wales: county boundaries since 1974*

areas and rateable values within the same category of authority, although much less than before 1974. Table 1 indicates the 1973 population ranges for each type of authority.

TABLE 1   *Population ranges for each type of authority in 1973*

Type of authority	Lowest population	Highest population
English metropolitan counties	1 198 390 (Tyne and Wear)	2 785 460 (West Midlands)
English non-metropolitan counties	109 680 (Isle of Wight)	1 434 960 (Kent)
Welsh counties	98 370 (Powys)	536 080 (Mid Glamorgan)
London boroughs	138 620 (Kingston upon Thames)	332 880 (Croydon)
English metropolitan districts	172 990 (South Tyneside)	1 087 660 (Birmingham)
English non-metropolitan districts	24 060 (Teeside)	421 800 (Avon)
Welsh districts	18 670 (Radnor)	285 760 (Cardiff)

SOURCE: NALGO Education Department

The reorganisation of local government in Scotland became effective on 1 April 1975 and resulted in the following very significant changes, under the Local Government (Scotland) Act 1973.

Structure prior to 1 April 1975		*Structure from 1 April 1975*	
County councils	33	Regional councils	9
Counties of cities	4	District councils	53
Large burghs	21	All-independent	
Small burghs	176	island authorities	3
Districts	198		
Total	432	Total	65

The revised local government structure in England and Wales is best summarised in diagrammatic form, as shown in Figure 4. The division of population in England between the three types of county council is: Greater London, 16 per cent; metropolitan counties, 25 per cent; and non-metropolitan counties, 59 per cent.

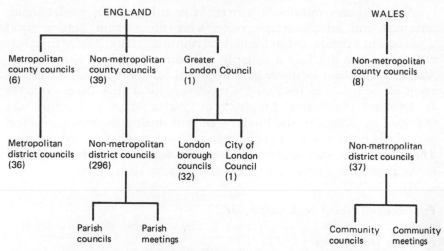

FIGURE. 4   *Revised local government structure — England and Wales*

Transitional Arrangements

Special temporary arrangements were needed to ensure a smooth transition from the old system to the new. In particular it was necessary to assemble resources of staff and accommodation, to establish suitable administrative arrangements and for the new councils to become familiar with their functions and activities.[5] Time was needed for the new councils to be elected and to take up their responsibilities and the 1972 Act provided a period of overlap during which the old and new councils existed side by side, although the new councils had no operational functions at that time.[4]

Prior to the elections of new councils, joint committees were set up for the new administrative areas composed of representatives of the appropriate existing authorities. Their brief was to prepare for the take-over by the new authorities and to assist in the co-ordination of policies on strategic matters, large-scale capital projects and other important issues. The joint committees were also encouraged to take basic management decisions, including those on committee and departmental structures, ideally adopting a corporate management approach as advocated in the Bains Report.[6]

One particularly difficult problem in the change-over period was the appointment of staff by the new local authorities. The main objectives were to redeploy existing staff in the most effective way, to protect the interests of staff and to assist the public by the smooth and efficient transfer of functions. In consequence the customary procedure of public advertisement was used only for a limited number of very senior posts, mainly chief executives to county councils and metropolitan districts. Most other senior professional, technical and administrative posts were filled from among local government officers within limited recruitment areas. Where this procedure did not produce a suitable applicant, the Local Government Staff Commission normally gave approval for the national advertisement of the post but restricted it to serving local government officers in England (excluding London) or Wales. This restriction was intended to safeguard the interests of staff during the reorganisation period when many posts were at risk and some might face redundancy. The majority of staff undertaking specific functions were transferred to the appropriate new authority without formal selection.

Functions of New Local Authorities

Discharge of Functions

Local authorities are statutory corporations created by Act of Parliament and limited in their activities to the powers and duties prescribed in the legislation. If they act unlawfully, the actions will be *ultra vires* (outside their powers) and the courts can prevent this. This aspect is considered in more detail in Chapter 8.

Local authority functions are of two main categories: those which they have a duty to perform (mandatory or compulsory functions); and those which they can perform at their discretion (permissive functions).

The majority of functions are compulsory – as, for instance, the provision of schools and teachers is a duty which an education authority is statutorily obliged to perform. On the other hand the provision of a museum is a service which many local authorities are empowered to provide if they believe it necessary, but there is no compulsion and it ranks as a permissive function.

Local authorities may also acquire additional powers under local Acts of Parliament, giving some measure of flexibility and enabling enterprising authorities to do pioneering work. Furthermore, authorities' functions vary over time, either by the allocation of new activities, such as consumer protection services, or by the transfer of functions to other bodies, such as water supply to the new water authorities.

All local authority services in any area of England and Wales can be provided by one or both of the principal councils, namely a metropolitan county and/or metropolitan district, a non-metropolitan county and/or non-metropolitan district, or the Greater London Council and/or a London borough. In some cases concurrent powers are exercised whereby some aspects of a service are provided at one level and other aspects at another, planning being one example. District councils can also in some instances undertake duties on behalf of county councils on an agency basis.

The underlying philosophy behind the division of local authority functions is to allocate to the counties those functions which need substantial resources and/or can be most effectively administered over large areas, such as strategic planning, major highways and police. At district council level, functions are allocated which are best provided in smaller units and where local knowledge and control are important, as with housing and local amenities.

Allocation of Functions

It is easier to understand the range and scope of local authority services if they are grouped in a meaningful way. Richards[5] has classified them into four groups.

1. *Protective* – protecting the individual from various dangers, through fire brigades, police forces, main drainage, refuse removal, food inspectors, weights and measures inspectors and the licensing of public premises.
2. *Communal* – for the benefit of all, such as the provision of roads and paths, street-lighting, planning and leisure services.
3. *Personal* – giving direct assistance to individuals, such as education and welfare services; this is now the most costly part of local authority services.
4. *Trading* – these have diminished with the nationalisation of gas and electricity undertakings and the transfer of water supply to the regional water authorities in 1974; nevertheless, there are some trading services remaining, such as public transport facilities and airports.

The allocation of services between the different categories of authority does not fit neatly into this grouping and the analysis of functions in this chapter is accordingly based on the following allocation groupings: mainly county; shared between county and district; additional functions of metropolitan districts; and mainly district.

County Councils

All county councils are highway authorities and have the principal responsibility for traffic regulation and transport functions. The Department of the Environment is responsible for trunk roads, although much of the operational work is delegated to county

councils, and major trunk and motorway projects are usually undertaken by road construction units staffed jointly from central and
local government. There are other exceptions to the general
provision – for instance, in Wales both on-street and off-street parking
are the responsibility of the district and in England both categories
of authority have responsibility for off-street parking. District
councils can claim responsibility for unclassified roads and the
London boroughs, including the City of London, are responsible
for non-metropolitan roads.

The councils of non-metropolitan counties have a duty to promote
co-ordinated and efficient passenger transport systems in their areas.
District councils operating bus undertakings have to operate in
accordance with county council policies and all operators are
required to co-operate with each other. Both county and district
councils can make grants towards the costs of public transport
operators.

Most police authorities are now amalgamated authorities but where
this has not occurred the county council is the local police authority.
County councils are fire authorities except where they are amalgamated authorities.

Except in the areas of joint boards, county councils formulate
strategic planning policy, prepare structure plans and decide on
'reserved' planning applications which impinge on county matters,
such as the disposal of mineral waste. With regard to National
Park areas most management and planning functions are allocated
to county councils, but there are some concurrent duties.

County councils in England are food and drug and local weights
and measures authorities, and are responsible for certain agricultural
services, but in some Welsh counties these powers may be vested
in district councils. In England district councils collect refuse and
county councils are responsible for disposal, while in Wales both collection and disposal rest with the district councils.

Shared Functions

There are some local authority functions which are shared between
county and district councils, as for instance the consideration of
planning applications and development control work generally,
and town development functions, while each authority is concerned
with specific aspects of the overall function. There are however many
other functions where both classes of authority are empowered to
provide the same service and this calls for a high level of co-
operation to avoid the duplication of expensive services.

Examples of services covered by concurrent powers are the

clearance of derelict land, the provision of caravan sites, and the provision and operation of country parks, swimming pools, parks and other open spaces, entertainment facilities such as theatres, concert halls and dance halls, physical training and recreation facilities, and museums and art galleries.

Additional Functions of Metropolitan Districts

There are a few very important and expensive services (education, social services and libraries) administered by non-metropolitan counties and metropolitan districts, which may at first sight appear a curious combination. It must however be remembered that the metropolitan districts are heavily populated, most of them being in the 200 000 to 300 000 population range, and they do accordingly have substantial resources.

Local education authorities are required by the Education Act 1944 to 'afford for all pupils opportunities for education offering such variety of instruction and training as may be desirable in view of their different ages, abilities and aptitudes, and of the different periods for which they may be expected to remain at school'. No fees are to be charged at schools maintained by local education authorities, except for board and lodging.

The statutory education system is divided into three distinct parts: primary education (children under 12); secondary education (12 to 19 years unless part of further education); and further education (young persons who have left school and adults). In addition, local education authorities have a duty to provide special schools for physically and mentally handicapped children.

Local education authorities also have powers to provide school meals services, holiday camps and swimming baths as part of physical training provision, boarding schools, nursery schools for children under five and youth service facilities to meet the recreational and social needs of young persons.

Non-metropolitan county and metropolitan district councils are required to provide a *social services committee* and appoint a director of social services to deal with a whole host of statutory social service functions. These functions include attending to the needs of children in care and the protection and welfare of children brought before the courts, which also involves the provision and operation of remand homes and approved schools, the supervision of children subject to court orders in matrimonial proceedings, the care of mothers and young children, domestic help, the prevention of illness and the care and after-care of the sick, the regulation

of nurseries and childminders, the provision of residential accommodation for the aged, infirm, needy and handicapped, and the
welfare of the handicapped and mentally disordered, and arranging
tasks for the chronically sick and disabled persons.

Finally, *library authorities* have a duty to provide a comprehensive
and efficient library service (Public Libraries and Museums Act
1964). In Wales some county councils and some district councils
are library authorities.

District Councils

The most important function of district councils is *housing*, with about
a quarter of the population housed in local authority dwellings.
The principal legislation is the Housing Act 1957, which places
a duty on housing authorities to ensure that all houses are fit for
human habitation and empowers them to make bye-laws regulating
overcrowding and the sanitary condition of houses. Housing
authorities can make clearance orders for groups of unfit houses.
Their primary function is however the provision of new dwellings,
and they can acquire land, manage dwellings and fix rents. They
can also make loans on mortgages for the purchase, building,
improvement and repair of dwellings for private occupation and
grants for the improvement of older dwellings. The 1964 Housing
Act gave local authorities the power to take over grossly mismanaged
houses in multiple occupation. County councils, except in Wales,
have reserve housing powers.

District councils also perform various *environmental or public health*
functions concerned with the abatement of nuisances, regulation of
offensive trades, such as bone, glue and blood processing, food
safety and hygiene, inspection of offices, shops and factories, control
of erection of new buildings and use of certain types of dwelling,
such as canal boats and common lodging houses, provision and
maintenance of local sewers, collection of refuse (disposal is a
county responsibility), street-cleansing, provision and maintenance
of public conveniences, baths and wash-houses, litter control and
enforcement of provisions of the Clean Air Act 1956.

All district councils remain the rating authorities and levy and
collect rates. They have complementary planning and highway
roles, as described previously. In addition district councils have
responsibilities, either individually or jointly, in connection with
the protection of the coast against erosion and encroachment by
the sea. They are empowered to provide and maintain markets,
cemeteries and crematoria, allotments, aerodromes, civic restaurants
and other trading services.

Parish and Community Councils

The powers of these authorities are very restricted and of limited significance. They include the provision and maintenance of allotments, burial grounds, public clocks, footpaths, bus shelters, recreation grounds, street-lighting and war memorials. They also have various powers relating to charities and common or parish land. A major function is to present local opinion to other local authorities and public bodies; they can, for instance, request to be consulted on local planning applications.[5]

Division of Responsibilities

Table 2 (see pages 42–3) shows in collated form the broad division of the principal local authority functions.

Problems in Operation of Latest Local Government Structure

The new local government structure is bound to create some operational problems. Probably the most likely source of friction is the shared and concurrent powers. Their satisfactory operation demands a high level of co-operation between counties and districts, which is not always achieved. The division of functions illustrated in Table 2 may appear confusing to the average elector and the existence of two or even three local authorities administering the same area may not give the impression of optimum effectiveness. It may also be argued that the two-tier structure leads to fragmentation and loss of a corporate approach.

Co-operation between counties and districts can be hindered by a variety of factors, such as local loyalties, party political differences and a natural tendency of district councils to strive for maximum independence. Members serving on both types of council may find their allegiance under strain on occasions when the policies of the two councils are in conflict.

Concurrent powers provide excellent opportunities for co-operation and teamwork. The practical effect can however be vastly different, with one authority waiting for the other to provide the particular service and the result that nothing is provided. Alternatively, both authorities may provide similar services in the same area causing unnecessary and expensive duplication. It is hoped that authorities will enter into mutual agreements for the provision of specific services or levels of services so that an integrated, adequate and efficient service is obtained.

With some services, such as highways and refuse disposal, it is possible for the district council to undertake county functions under

TABLE 2 *Division of English local government functions*

Category	Function	County		District	
		Metropolitan	Non-metropolitan	Metropolitan	Non-metropolitan
Mainly county	*Highways and transportation*				
	Transport planning	F	F	–	–
	Highways	F	F	Clmd	Clmd
	Traffic	F	F	–	–
	Parking	F	F	PF	PF
	Public transport	F	Co-ordn	–	Opertn
	Road safety	F	F	–	–
	Aerodromes	CP	CP	CP	CP
	Protective services				
	Police	F/Amls	F/Amls	–	–
	Fire	F/Amls	F/Amls	–	–
	Consumer protection	F	F	–	–
	Planning				
	Structure plans	F	F	–	–
Shared services	*Planning, amenity and leisure*				
	Local plans	–	–	F	F
	Development control	SF	SF	SF	SF
	Town development	SF	SF	SF	SF
	Acquisition and development of land	SF	SF	SF	SF
	Clearance of derelict land	CP	CP	CP	CP
	Country parks	CP	CP	CP	CP
	Footpaths and bridleways	SF	SF	SF	SF
	Caravan sites (provision)	CP	CP	CP	CP
	Swimming baths	CP	CP	CP	CP
	Parks and open spaces	CP	CP	CP	CP
	Entertainments	CP	CP	CP	CP

Additional metropolitan district functions

Mainly district

	C1	C2	C3	C4
Physical training and recreation	CP	CP	CP	CP
Museums and art galleries	CP	CP	CP	CP
Personal services				
Education	—	F	F	—
Social services	—	F	F	—
Libraries	—	F	F	—
Housing				
Provision, improvement and clearance	Res	Res	F	F
Health and environment				
Public health duties	—	—	F	F
Local sewers	—	—	F	F
Litter control	—	—	F	F
Clean air enforcement	—	—	F	F
Coast protection	—	—	F	F
Unclassified roads	—	—	F	F
Street-cleansing	—	—	F	F
Cemeteries and crematoria	—	—	F	F
Markets	—	—	F	F
Refuse collection	F	F	F	F
Refuse disposal	—	F	F	—
Allotments	—	—	F	F

NOTE: This schedule is not conclusive as there are variations in the allocation of functions in London and Wales, as described in the text.

KEY

F	function or service undertaken	CP	concurrent powers
Amls	subject to amalgamations	PF	partial function or power
Clmd	certain powers can be claimed	SF	shared function

Co-ordn co-ordination
Opertn operation
Res reserve

an agency arrangement with the county council. Agency arrangements do not always operate smoothly, as the lower-level authority is placed in a subordinate position acting under the control and subject to the scrutiny of the county council. There is a loss of freedom of action and this can lead to resentment on the part of the district council.

The area most likely to give rise to problems is that of planning, where powers are shared between county and district councils. In essence, counties formulate broad policy or strategy and the districts are responsible for the detailed application of county policy to local developments. Failure by districts to apply county policy to their individual decisions can undermine this policy. The more important development applications are termed 'county matters' and are reserved for county decision but disputes can arise in defining 'county matters'. A high level of co-operation and mutual confidence is essential to the effective administration of this service.

Further Transfer of Functions from Local Government

Local government activity in the National Health Service was largely eliminated on 1 April 1974, when the health service was reorganised by the establishment of *ad hoc* regional and area health authorities, which were planned to coincide with the creation of the new metropolitan district and non-metropolitan county councils. The medical officer of health in the local government service ceased to be a statutory officer.

At the same time ten regional water authorities were created with responsibility for water conservation and supply, pollution and sewage treatment. This resulted in the transfer of water supply and sewage treatment functions from local authorities to the new bodies.

References

1. Cmnd. 4584, *Local Government in England: Government Proposals for Reorganisation* (H.M.S.O., 1971).
2. Cmnd. 4583, *Reform of Local Government in Scotland* (H.M.S.O., 1971).
3. WELSH OFFICE, *The Reform of Local Government in Wales* (H.M.S.O., 1971).
4. HART, W. O. and GARNER, J. F., *Hart's Introduction to the Law of Local Government and Administration* (Butterworth, 1973).
5. RICHARDS, P. G., *The Reformed Local Government System* (Allen and Unwin, 1975).

6. STUDY GROUP ON LOCAL AUTHORITY MANAGEMENT STRUCTURES, *The New Local Authorities: Management and Structure* – the Bains Report (H.M.S.O., 1972).

CHAPTER FOUR

LOCAL GOVERNMENT PROCEDURES

Constitution of Local Authorities

Local authorities are independent administrative bodies created by and exercising functions conferred by Parliament. Nevertheless, certain Ministers of State have power to direct local authorities in the exercise of their duties. The Minister with prime responsibility for local government is the Secretary of State for the Environment, hereinafter referred to as the Minister.

The Local Government Act 1972 prescribes the constitution of the principal councils (county and district councils) in England and Wales.

1. *County councils* comprise a chairman and vice-chairman, both of whom are elected at the annual meeting of the county council from among the councillors, and a number of county councillors, who are elected by ballot in the manner described later in this chapter. County councillors serve for a period of four years and retire simultaneously, but are free to stand for re-election.

2. *County district councils* comprise a chairman and vice-chairman, both of whom are elected at the annual meeting of the council from among the councillors, and a number of district councillors, who are directly elected by the electors for a period of four years. In the case of metropolitan district councils one-third of the councillors in each ward retire annually in rotation, except that in the county council election year there is no election for district councillors. Non-metropolitan district councils can choose either to hold an election for all councillors once every four years on the county council pattern, or to adopt the metropolitan district council procedure of partial renewal by thirds. Where a district is designated as a borough, the chairman becomes mayor but his functions do not differ from those of a chairman. The granting of borough status permits the preservation of any special privileges of a ceremonial nature which may have been granted in earlier charters to the predecessors of the new borough.[1]

3. *Parishes and communities* In addition to the parish councils and meetings based on the old rural parishes, many new ones resulted from the operation of the Local Government Act 1972. Some of the new parishes were formerly boroughs and districts which

are now enmeshed by larger non-metropolitan county districts. Other new parishes have been formed from groupings of former parishes. The fundamental unit of local government in an English parish or Welsh community is the meeting of all local government electors for the area. This takes place annually or twice a year where there is no parish council. Where there is a parish council, the chairman of the council presides at parish meetings, otherwise the meeting annually chooses a chairman.[1] Most parishes have an elected council, holding office for four years and retiring simultaneously.

4. *The Greater London Council* consists of a chairman and councillors, but can also appoint a vice-chairman and deputy chairman. The councillors represent single-member electoral divisions, hold office for three years and retire simultaneously.

5. *London borough councils* are 32 in number and each comprises a mayor and councillors. The councillors hold office for three years and retire simultaneously.

6. *The City Corporation* administers an area of approximately one square mile (2.6 square kilometres) in the centre of London. The Corporation acts through three courts:

   (i) The Court of Common Hall consisting of liverymen, who are freemen of the city.

   (ii) The Court of Aldermen is in essence a 'second chamber', which is exceptional in local government and consists of 26 aldermen elected for life by the electors for the respective wards.

   (iii) The Court of Common Council is the principal governing body and consists of the Lord Mayor, aldermen and 159 common councillors. The councillors are elected annually by the electors.

Election Qualifications

A candidate for election to a local authority must:

1. be a British national or a citizen of the Irish Republic and be at least 21 years of age:

2. possess *one* of the following qualifications identifying the candidate with the particular area:

   (i) be registered as a local government elector for the area of the authority; or

   (ii) have occupied land or premises in that area as owner or tenant during the whole of the preceding twelve months; or

(iii) have had his principal or only place of work in that area during the whole of the preceding twelve months; or

(iv) have resided in that area during the whole of the preceding twelve months; or

(v) in the case of a parish or community council, have resided either in the parish or community or within 3 miles (4.83 kilometres) of it during the whole of the preceding twelve months.

The following disqualifications also apply to intending and existing councillors:

1. holding a paid office or employment appointed by the local authority or any of its committees, other than a chairman or vice-chairman who may receive allowances;
2. being adjudged bankrupt or making a composition with creditors;
3. being surcharged by a district auditor for an amount exceeding £500 within five years before or since election;
4. being convicted in the United Kingdom for any offence with a term of imprisonment of not less than three months without the option of a fine, within five years before or since election;
5. being guilty of corrupt and illegal practices at an election;
6. consequent upon an audit of local authority accounts, a court may by order disqualify a member who has incurred or authorised expenditure exceeding £2000 which was contrary to law.[1]

Election Procedures

Local Government Franchise

Councillors are elected by secret ballot by local government electors for the local authority area. The qualifications for entry to the register of local government electors derive mainly from the Representation of the People Acts 1949 and 1969.

The right to vote at a local authority election is conferred upon British subjects and citizens of the Republic of Ireland who are at least 18 years of age at the date of the poll, who are not subject to any legal incapacity to vote, and whose names appear on the appropriate register of local government electors. Electors must be resident in the local authority area on the 'qualifying date' (10 October).

The register is reviewed annually from dwelling occupiers' declarations under the direction of the electoral registration officer, who is often the chief executive to the local authority. Registers come into effect on 16 February each year, although a preliminary register is available earlier when those omitted can apply for inclusion and objections are heard by the registration officer, with right of appeal to the County Court and thence to the Court of Appeal. Local government electors are entitled to vote at all council elections (county, district and parish) appertaining to their area.

For election purposes, county council areas are subdivided into districts known as electoral divisions, and in the case of district councils and London boroughs the divisions are known as wards. Each electoral division in a county returns one councillor, while non-metropolitan district council wards normally return three councillors but this may be varied to suit local conditions. The number of councillors returned by the wards of metropolitan districts is divisible by three.

Conduct of Elections

The conduct of local government elections is the responsibility of a returning officer. Each county council appoints a returning officer for county council elections and each district council appoints a returning officer for the district and for the parishes or communities within it.

The returning officer commences the election proceedings by issuing a Notice of Election. He ensures that all statutory requirements are met and arranges the provision and manning of polling stations, the counting of votes, decides disputed ballot papers and declares the results.

Candidates' nomination papers must be signed by a proposer, a seconder and eight other electors for the area and be handed to the returning officer by noon on the nineteenth day preceding the election (nomination day). Nomination papers for parish council elections can be restricted to a proposer and seconder. Nominations must contain the candidate's consent to stand, attested by a witness, and a statement of the candidate's qualification for election. Both nomination and ballot papers may contain a description of the candidate of not more than six words, including political affiliations. The returning officer examines the nomination papers, determines the validity of the nominations and subsequently publishes a list of candidates.

Each candidate may appoint an election agent to manage his campaign, although he can act as his own agent provided he notifies the returning officer at least twelve days prior to the election. Where the number of nominations equals or is less than the vacancies, then no election is required. In the latter case the returning officer declares the candidates elected and fills the remaining vacancies with the retiring councillors who received the highest number of votes at the previous election.

Where the number of nominations exceeds the vacancies, a poll of electors by ballot is arranged on election day. The candidate's agent and voluntary workers endeavour to obtain support for their candidate by displaying posters, canvassing electors, arranging election meetings and acting as polling or counting agents on election day. Various practices are prohibited such as the indiscriminate display of posters, harassment, bribery and financing of cars to carry electors to and from the polls. The candidate and his agent must record all election expenditure and keep within the statutory limit.[2]

Within two months of election a councillor must deliver a written acceptance of office to the appropriate officer of the council, otherwise a vacancy will be created. Complaints of alleged irregularities at local government elections are made by election petition addressed to an election court, which consists of a commissioner appointed by the Judges of the High Court.

Casual Vacancies

A casual vacancy may arise through the death, disqualification or retirement of a councillor. A councillor who fails to attend a meeting for six months without the council's approval is deemed to have vacated his seat. Casual vacancies are filled at by-elections – conducted in a similar manner to ordinary elections – except where the casual vacancy occurs within six months of the date of the next ordinary election, when it is left unfilled.

Alteration of Local Government Areas

Two permanent Local Government Boundary Commissions, for England and Wales respectively, were established by the Local Government Act 1972. Each Commission consists of a chairman, deputy chairman and several members (five for England and three for Wales), all appointed by the appropriate Secretary of State.

These Commissions have a primary duty to keep all local government boundaries under constant review, following a relatively simple and informal procedure based on consultation. Their recommendations to become operative have to be confirmed by orders made by the Secretary of State. English reviews are to be undertaken at intervals of ten to fifteen years, but no time interval has been prescribed for Wales. Each Commission also has to review electoral arrangements for all principal areas at intervals of ten to fifteen years.

District councils are to keep under review the boundaries and electoral arrangements of parishes and communities and to make recommendations, where appropriate, to the relevant Commission. Where a district council refuses or neglects to consider a request for review from a parish or community council, the Commission may, on being approached, make recommendations to the district council.

Councils and their Meetings

Members of local authorities have various rights, one of which is to attend council meetings, but have no absolute right to be a member of any specific committee. They cannot be removed from office while they remain qualified to serve. Members also acquire obligations: for instance, they must declare any pecuniary interest in any contract or other matter under discussion and not vote on it. They are also liable to be surcharged if they vote for unlawful expenditure.

The Local Government Act 1972 prescribes procedural arrangements for meetings, notice required, number of members to constitute a quorum, method of voting and like matters. Decisions on ordinary business must be made by a majority of the members present. Minutes of meetings must be available for inspection by local government electors and the Act reaffirms that the press and other members of the public shall be admitted to full council and committee meetings, although they can be excluded from parts where the council considers it to be in the public interest. Local authorities may make standing orders prescribing rules of conduct for council and committee meetings.

Councils often have a large membership and the Bains Report[4] questioned the effectiveness of large councils for management purposes. Jones[5] suggests that the main function of a council is not management but representation. He believes its primary role is to deliberate, criticise and ratify, and a widely representative body is needed to carry out these activities successfully. Many of the council's functions are discharged through committees and officers, but subject to policies and decisions of the council.

Management in Local Government

Prior to local government reorganisation in 1974, most local authorities were structured on the basis of departments operating

under the direction and control of committees, which prepared
budgets and thus became competitors for their share of the total
available resources. The larger authorities provide a wide range
of services which are interrelated and hence no one service should
be treated in isolation.

The Bains Report[4] placed great emphasis on the corporate
approach to management in local government, believing that the
traditional departmental procedure was no longer appropriate to
secure the most effective use of resources. Hence the study group
recommended that management activities be concentrated in a policy
and resources committee supported by a chief executive and a
management team of officers. In this way an authority can formulate
more realistically its long-term objectives covering all services,
and make forward planning projections, decisions as to priorities
and assessments of financial implications.

The basic philosophy is that at policy stage councillors decide
and officers advise, while at the ensuing execution stage councillors
monitor and officers perform. This represents an oversimplification,
as policy and administration cannot always be clearly distinguished
and the boundaries can become blurred. The administration of
policy frequently concerns the councillor more significantly than
the policy itself. The electors' worries, as relayed to the councillor,
usually stem from policy implementation, be it housing, highways,
schools, libraries, town planning or whatever, and particularly how
it affects them as individuals. Furthermore, a councillor is better
able to assist in making policy if he is aware of how it will work
in practice, and of its implications and consequences.[5] Corporate
management is considered in more detail in Chapter 5.

Committee Structure

Functions of Committees

The committee system is a characteristic feature of English local
government, whereby the work of the local authority is subdivided
between groups of councillors, sometimes supported by co-opted
persons, and smaller in size than the whole council. The Local
Government Act 1972 gave local authorities a discretionary power
to set up committees, joint committees and sub-committees to enable
them to discharge their functions. This Act gave local authorities
greater freedom in the organisation of their internal structures, and
many have streamlined their committee systems by setting up a policy
or management committee and reducing the number of committees.[1]

The committee system enables multi-purpose authorities to deal
with their work effectively. The wide range of functions and variety

of detailed matters requiring decision by the principal authorities could not be handled at full council level without massive delegation to paid officers, which would destroy the democratic principle and result in councils being no more than rubber stamps. Committees comprise a council's workshops, where officers' technical knowledge and councillors' assessments of public needs are integrated and a balanced solution formulated.[6]

Types of Committee

Committees can be classified in the following way.

1. *Statutory and permissive* Statutory committees are those which local authorities are by statute compelled to set up, namely the education committee of a local education authority, the police committee of a county police authority and the social services committee of a social services authority. Permissive committees are those which a local authority is not compelled to establish but can do so if it wishes.

2. *Standing and special* Standing committees are set up on a relatively permanent basis and are normally renewed annually. Special committees are set up to deal with specific short-term matters, such as extensions to council offices or a review of house-improvement policy, and are disbanded when the objective has been realised.

3. *Service and machinery* Service committees administer services or functions of a local authority, such as leisure services or highways. Machinery or co-ordinative committees are concerned with administrative machinery such as finance and personnel.

Joint committees can be appointed by two or more local authorities to deal with matters of common interest. This arrangement offers considerable flexibility and is ideally suited to the management of such facilities as airports and sports centres in which more than one authority has an interest.[3]

Joint boards consist of the nominees of two or more authorities and they administer a service in which the appointing authorities have a mutual interest. They differ from joint committees in that they are separate from and independent of their constituent authorities, and are almost invariably bodies corporate with a perpetual existence and their own financial powers.[1] Typical examples would be joint education boards and joint planning boards set up by the appropriate ministers.

Composition and Size of Committees

The Local Government Act 1972 enabled local authorities to decide the number of members on committees, their term of office and any limitations on powers delegated to them. Committees make similar decisions in respect of their sub-committees.

Finance committees must always consist entirely of members of the appointing council. Other committees may consist wholly or partly of councillors, but at least two-thirds of them must be members of the appointing local authority.

Varying opinions have been expressed as to the desirable size of committees from small to large. The main advantage of a small committee is believed to be expeditious dispatch of business. Advocates of large committees expound the benefits of better representation of sectional interests and areas, and adequate representation when some members are absent.

Sub-committees may be appointed to relieve main committees of routine work or to deal with specialist or complicated issues. For example, in education it is common practice to establish separate sub-committees to deal with primary, secondary and further education respectively, which in their turn may appoint sectional sub-committees to handle specific aspects, such as appointment of teaching staff and award of grants. The recommendations of Maud[7] and Bains[4] if adopted would largely eliminate sub-committees by transferring their work to officers.

Control of Committees by Council

Committees are ultimately answerable to the council whatever the arrangements adopted, which may be varied through party politics or local traditions. There are three main criteria.

1. A council cannot delegate the function of levying or issuing a precept for a rate or borrowing money. For instance, a statutory county police committee is obliged to submit its financial estimates to the county council, which then includes the appropriate details in its precepts.
2. Matters may be delegated to a committee which then has power to act on behalf of the council, but the committee will report its actions to the council. Most committees have a wide measure of delegated authority on matters which do not involve new policy, thus ensuring the expeditious dispatch of business and a suitable division of duties between a council and its committees. Functions can also be delegated to sub-committees and officers.
3. Matters may be referred to a committee to consider and report

back to the council which may adopt, amend or reject the recommendations.

Co-option

The Local Government Act 1972 empowers a local authority to co-opt members from outside the authority to any committee, other than one for regulating and controlling finance. A co-opted member has the same rights and privileges on the committee as an elected member, and has the same voting powers and the same obligations, such as the disclosure of interests in contracts.

This procedure provides the means of obtaining expert and specialised advice. The Maud Committee[7] found that about two-thirds of co-opted members represented groups or bodies, thereby promoting co-operation and mutual understanding, and about one-third were appointed in a personal capacity.

Committee Arrangements

The flow of business is initiated by an officer deciding to channel business through a committee rather than dealing with it administratively. As described earlier it is not always easy to distinguish between administrative and policy issues. An important administrative matter such as the reorganisation of a department may have policy implications, while a policy matter may be so insignificant that it would not warrant consideration by a committee. The size of the authority can also influence the decision, as committees of small authorities will normally consider more detailed matters than those of larger authorities. The experience, personality and approach of principal officers will also affect the practice adopted.

Committee meetings must be held reasonably frequently to avoid excessive delay in dealing with business, but not so frequently that members are called to meetings with little to discuss. Most of the authorities that once worked to a monthly cycle now meet at six-week intervals, accompanied by increased delegation of functions to committees and authority to officers.

An orderly sequence of meetings is vital as some committees, such as finance and establishment, have to consider recommendations from other committees and must therefore follow them. There must be adequate time between committee meetings and prior to the council meeting for submission of minutes and reports. All meetings are normally timetabled in advance in a council yearbook and/or diary of meetings.

It should be noted that committees can be organised both horizontally and vertically. Service committiees, such as education and highways, operate vertically in a line down from council, to committee, to department, to the public. Committees responsible for internal functions, such as finance and personnel, have a line of activity across the authority and not down to the public.[8]

Most important business flows upward to the council[9] and comprises mainly the consideration of minutes and reports from committees, reports by officers, communications from other authorities and notices of motion by members of the council. Various constitutional matters, including the election of the chairman or mayor, are dealt with at the annual meeting of a local authority.

Advantages of the Committee System

1. The establishment of suitable committees, properly programmed, ensures that matters can be dealt with concurrently and the flow of business expedited.
2. Matters of detail can be fully discussed in committee leaving the major policy issues to be decided in full council.
3. Some measure of flexibility is secured with new committees being established or old ones discontinued as circumstances and needs change.
4. At committee meetings members can speak more freely than at a council meeting, compromise decisions on controversial matters are more easily made, officers are better able to offer advice and minor but nonetheless worrying issues of electors can be discussed and decided.
5. Councillors become conversant with particular council services or functions and are able to contribute to their development, to gain an understanding of the consequences of policies and so improve the soundness of their decisions, and to understand and appreciate opposing viewpoints.

Disadvantages of the Committee System

1. Decisions tend to be slowed down and are more likely to lead to compromise solutions.
2. Too much time may be spent on relatively minor issues.
3. The system may give rise to fragmentation and compartmentalism and involve cumbersome and inefficient procedures.
4. Councillors may exaggerate the importance of their committees, so cutting across a corporate approach.

Later Developments of the Committee System

The Maud Committee[7] believed that council work was fragmented excessively by the committee structure and disliked the committee/

department relationship. The Committee advocated the recasting of committees under a formulatory, supervisory and executive management board, although this concept proved unacceptable to local authorities. The Maud Committee also advocated a reduced size and number of committees.

The subsequent Bains Study Group[4] advocated a policy and resources committee with a planning, co-ordinating, monitoring and controlling role, advising the council, which would operate primarily as a debating and policy-making forum. Finance, personnel, land and performance review sub-committees could deal with more routine aspects. The study group also advocated the delineation of programme areas each with its own programme committee, covering groupings of services such as education, planning and transportation, public protection, and amenities in counties, and development services, leisure and recreation, environmental health, and housing in districts.

Councillors

Characteristics

Councillors are basically ordinary citizens who devote part of their time to the service of local authorities. They do not draw salaries but can be paid allowances for loss of working time and to cover the cost of travelling and subsistence.

The composition of councils although covering a wide spectrum differs from the groupings in the country as a whole. Certain groups such as younger persons, women, and skilled and unskilled workers are underrepresented. The business of local authorities occupies a considerable amount of time and the work of the larger authorities has become more arduous and complex. Many meetings are held during the day, when many workers and professional men are unable to attend.

Traditionally local authorities were dominated by the wealthier classes, but in more recent times people with smaller business interests and professional people have increasingly been elected to councils. The growth of the labour movement has resulted in an influx of trade union officials, political agents and a variety of other occupations. Nevertheless in 1964 the average age of councillors was 55 and only 12 per cent of councillors were women. One-fifth of all members were retired people.

Qualities

Councillors receive little monetary return for all the effort and time they expend on behalf of their authorities. In these materialistic times many electors find it difficult to believe that members' prime concern is the welfare of the community and the desire to render public service. It is frequently suggested, with little or no real evidence, that most members gain indirectly through their businesses and professions, despite the fact that many councillors have no interests of these kinds.

Councillors are in practice motivated by a variety of factors – a form of self-expression, a hobby, an interest, a means of influencing local affairs or a wish to enter public life – all culminating in an enriching and satisfying experience.[6] The transaction of business in open council means that councillors' actions are subject to public scrutiny, and this generally ensures that they pay attention to public opinion.

Functions

The primary functions of all councillors ought desirably to be the direction and control of council affairs, making key decisions, monitoring progress and the broad supervision of officers and their work to ensure that agreed policy is implemented, that ratepayers secure value for money and that there is an absence of waste or graft. It is the duty of councillors to investigate complaints lodged by members of the public and to elicit the facts.

The Bains Study Group[4] attempted an analysis of the main aims and interests of councillors and suggested five categories – namely that members may be interested in broad policy, welfare activities, management along commercial lines, service to the community, or limiting spending, but these may be affected by the type of authority and political affiliations.

In contrast, Jones[5] has suggested three broad categories: the representative – the spokesman and watchdog (about 75 per cent); the specialised policy-maker – concerned with one or two services or functions (about 20 per cent); and the broad policy-maker – concerned with the overall policy of the local authority and establishing priorities (about 5 per cent).

Jones has also described how the representative function could be divided into a geographical area, such as a ward, a section of the community, such as property owners or council house tenants, an organised group with political, social, professional or other interests, another local authority in a tier arrangement, or individual citizens. All councillors perform this function to some extent, usually related to specific detailed matters appertaining to policy administration.

The position of the individual councillor is both unusual and confusing. He has no real identity except as part of the council; he cannot as an individual give instructions to officers, visit council properties or even, in the majority of cases, examine council files. A council normally takes action by resolution and cannot generally delegate functions to individual members, except committee chairmen. Mallaby[10] makes the interesting assertion that 'if local government is to survive as a distinctive and positive force, councillors, by their wisdom and efficiency, must prove that they are in fact an essential and lively part of the constitution'.

Pay and Allowances

Because of the rather depressed status of local government in the eyes of a lot of people, many employers do not regard it sufficiently important to participate in or to permit their employees to do so. The Maud Committee[7] recognised this problem and recommended employers to release employees to serve on councils. Some have advocated paying councillors a salary but this proposal has been largely rejected mainly on the grounds that it would attract persons who were motivated by less sincere reasons and destroy the voluntary tradition of local government.

Councils can pay councillors attendance allowances for approved duty and, in 1977, these were generally in the order of £5 to £8 for a four-hour period or half-day, or £10 for a longer period up to one day. The allowances are calculated on a door-to-door basis to include travelling time. They are not dependent for payment upon loss of earnings, but are claimable as of right whenever a councillor performs an approved duty. In addition travel and subsistence allowances are payable on prescribed statutory scales.

Party Politics in Local Government

Party politics now operate to a significant extent in local government and are applied with varying degrees of rigidity. This move had its foundations in the last century, when left-wing reformers saw the opportunity of securing local reforms, of financing candidates from the working classes out of party funds and later of establishing local Labour councils to support the party's national policies. Since the Second World War the Conservatives have become more openly active in local government, followed in the last two decades by increasing Liberal Party activity.

The party system is at its strongest in the larger urban areas and is at its weakest in rural areas. Local government reorganisation resulted in a reduction in the percentage of independent seats on county councils from 39.5 per cent in 1970 to 14.3 per cent in 1974.

Many opposing arguments are put forward on the desirability or otherwise of operating party politics in local government. Supporters contend that national and local issues are inseparable and that effective planning and administration can be achieved only through a consistent policy operated over a period of years. Large councils, so it is argued, are bound to act as groups and when a group represents a local party it is elected on a clearly defined programme and is more responsive to public opinion. Probably the strongest case can be made in larger authorities where many complicated issues arise.

Opponents argue that what is mainly needed in local government is sound common-sense solutions to practical problems which have little direct relevance to party policies and ideologies. Carried to extremes party politics can result in all policy matters being decided outside the council chamber by a local party group, making the council meeting a mere formality and extinguishing the debating and questioning activities in committees. There is a danger that the national headquarters of a political party might exert excessive influence on local council proceedings and rigid party discipline might be applied in the most inappropriate situations.

The Maud Committee[7] recognised these dangers and believed that party politics were to be deplored if they produced irrelevant and sterile debate, stifled discussion or dictated an approach towards issues which were essentially non-political. Whilst recognising that party politics formed an inescapable part of public life, the Committee commented unfavourably on the possible increased dependence of local authorities on central government resulting from the close association of political parties at national and local level. It was believed the local authorities would benefit from having some members without party affiliations.

Officers

Few councillors can devote all their time to council business, which is becoming increasingly technical and complex, and hence they are concerned primarily with deciding principles and policies. Full-time salaried officers are accordingly appointed to give expert advice, carry out the day-to-day work of administration and execute policy.

Principal Responsibilities

To undertake their various functions, local authorities employ officers covering a wide range of specialisms from lawyers and accountants to environmental health officers and teachers. Some are trained in the local government service while others enter the service fully qualified. The recruitment and training of officers is considered in more detail in Chapter 6.

Each major council service or group of related services is normally administered by a department under a highly experienced chief officer. Some departments comprise a range of personnel in the professional, administrative, clerical and manual categories, undertaking work varying from day-to-day administration to the execution of major capital schemes. Staffing arrangements vary enormously between different authorities with their wide differences in areas, populations and functions. There are two broad classifications of employee – 'officers', who undertake professional, administrative and clerical duties, and 'servants', who do manual work.

Under the Local Government Act 1972, local authorities have a duty to appoint 'such officers as they think necessary for the proper discharge . . . of their functions . . . on such reasonable terms and conditions, including conditions as to remuneration,' as the appointing authority thinks fit.

The local government officer is largely bound by the normal master/servant relationship and must give loyal and effective service, carry out all reasonable and lawful instructions and steadfastly avoid being bribed or corrupted. Employment in the public service places special obligations upon officers in that they have a statutory duty to account satisfactorily for all monies and properties in their charge, they must notify the authority in writing of any pecuniary interest in council contracts or other relevant matters, and must not as officers exact or accept any fee or reward[6] or authorise or perform any illegal acts.

The primary function of a local government officer is to advise and to carry out the lawful instructions of his council, including performing delegated functions. Chief officers may from time to time find their advice in conflict with the majority view of councillors and they should proceed with tact and firmness. Jackson[6] has described how 'the art of public administration consists, to a considerable extent, in reconciling and harmonizing conflicting interests'. Hart and Garner[1] have emphasised how officers, when tendering expert advice to elected members, must avoid becoming identified with party political views: they must not appear publicly to be making decisions which are the subject of political controversy.

The principal officer to a principal authority is usually designated the chief executive, and he acts as controller and co-ordinator of the authority's staff and functions. The Maud Report[7] identified the chief executive as a team leader and co-ordinator and as a focal point for unity of direction at officer level. The Bains Report[4] pursued the same theme with the chief executive identified as the head of the authority's paid service with authority over the principal officers and freed from departmental responsibilities. With local government reorganisation in 1974, the majority of principal authorities appointed executives freed from departmental responsibilities and only one continued with the traditional clerk/solicitor arrangement. Some however compromised by appointing a chief executive with departmental responsibilities and others have changed to this arrangement since reorganisation.

Statutory Officers

Apart from the general power to appoint officers derived from the Local Government Act 1972, local authorities are required by certain statutes to appoint specific officers, known as 'statutory officers', and the principal ones are now listed.

1. The Chief Education Officer of non-metropolitan county and metropolitan district councils (Education Act 1944).
2. The Chief Fire Officer of a county council (Fire Services Act 1947).
3. The Chief Inspector of Weights and Measures of English county councils and Welsh district councils (Weights and Measures Act 1963).
4. The Chief Constable of county and combined police forces (Police Act 1964).
5. The Director of Social Services of non-metropolitan county and metropolitan district councils (Local Authority Social Services Act 1970).

The Local Government Act 1933 required county and borough councils to appoint a clerk, treasurer and surveyor, but the 1972 Act and the Bains Report[4] has rather changed the situation. There are some other statutory officers such as district surveyors to the Greater London Council, who enforce the London Building Acts and Constructional By-laws. Reorganisation of the National Health Service in 1974 resulted in the statutory appointment of Medical Officer of Health being replaced by the Chief Community Physician of the area health authority.

Some statutory officers have security of tenure of office in that their appointment and/or dismissal require ratification by a Minister of State. For instance, a Chief Education Officer's dismissal requires confirmation by the Secretary of State for Education and Science, while the Secretary of State for Home Affairs has to approve the appointment and dismissal of Chief Constables and the appointment of Chief Fire Officers.

Relationship of Members and Officers

The officer is strictly speaking the servant of the council and must carry out all lawful instructions of the council. He must implement the policies formulated by the council irrespective of his own views on them. Nevertheless this broad subdivision of council activity into policy determination and its subsequent execution oversimplifies a complex system. Furthermore the councillor/officer relationship differs from the normal master/servant situation because of the professional advice that officers give, which often influences decisions made by members, and their important administrative role.

The Maud Committee[7] believed that members should take and be responsible for key decisions on objectives, and on the means and plans to achieve them, while officers should give the necessary advice. This recommendation received little support. The Bains Study Group[4] doubted the practicability of dividing the management process in this way and saw the analogy of a scale – 'as one moves through the management scale, the balance between the two elements changes from member control with officer advice at the objective end to officer control with member advice at the execution end'.

Jones[5] has described how administrative detail can embrace aspects of policy and how policy itself frequently stems from an accumulation of detailed decisions. Members generally do not want to be restricted to policy formulation as they need to be aware of the problems of implementation, and it would be equally wrong to confine officers to administration as they have so much to contribute to policy-making as a result of their immense experience and expertise. Contributions of members and officers should be interlinked at all stages in the interests of democracy and efficiency.

Officers hold permanent appointments and should not handle potentially publicly controversial matters which could, following a change in the majority party, adversely affect their careers. Close working relationships are bound to develop between senior officers and the appropriate committee chairmen, whatever their politics. Senior officers must be free to report to and advise committees on all matters coming within their purview and this constitutes one of the greatest strengths of English local government. As described earlier in this chapter, officers not only give information and expert advice to committees but also assist in shaping plans and guiding policy, and may on occasions even warn against excessive inertia or over-ambitious experiment. Hence the Bains recom-

mendation urging members and officers 'to forge an effective
partnership'.[4]

Grugeon[11] has described how a chief officer is relatively secure
and amply supported with detailed information on the entire working
of his service. By contrast the political service committee chairman
knows only what the chief officer has told him, and is much more
insecure. The chairman can move only at a speed dictated by his
political colleagues and acceptable to the electorate. Grugeon
believes that there is room for occasional disagreement but it is
important that there shall never be a gulf in communication between
the two sides of the partnership.

Corruption

All local government committees of inquiry during the 1960s and
1970s have affirmed that the majority of members and officers are
honest, despite the frequent references to bribery and corruption
in local government by television, radio and the press. It is essential
that this is so as once the public doubts the integrity of local government, central government could feel justified in exercising greater
control of or even removing more functions from local authorities.[12]

Jones[12] advocates constant vigilance and the need for leading
members and senior officers to maintain and ensure the highest
standards. He also identifies the greatest danger as 'unchecked
power', where a powerful committee chairman works closely with
a very strong chief officer in making important decisions. Such
arrangements are even more dangerous when one party or group
has an overwhelming majority and controls all committees.

Both members and officials must in their own interests exercise
the greatest care when engaging consultants, awarding contracts or
deciding planning applications, to leave no room for public
criticism. They must be particularly wary of offers of an 'all-in
service' which are claimed to provide a more efficient and faster
service, and of which the Poulson integrated architectural practice
with its trail of corrupt contacts is an unhappy reminder. Standing
orders and procedures operate as important safeguards in ensuring
that public money is not mis-spent.

Herbert Morrison in the years between the wars advocated good,
honest local government. He particularly advised that members
and officers should not become too friendly, there being no exchange
of hospitality or favours, use of first names should be avoided and
all business conducted at the office. Contractors should be kept
beyond arm's length to prevent personal interests affecting public
decisions, while recognising that in most towns they are bound to

meet socially through a variety of associations. Finally both senior members and officers must themselves maintain the highest standards and ensure that their colleagues do the same.

In the early 1970s some leading local authority members and senior officers, who had given so much devoted service to local government, were found guilty of corrupt practices, which were as unnecessary as they were unfortunate. It is incumbent on all local authorities to operate adequate and effective checking devices to eliminate as far as practicable illegal expenditure, waste, extravagance and inefficient administration. To keep this aspect in perspective, evidence suggests that there is far less corruption now than a hundred years ago, despite the enormous increase in size and complexity of the local government service.

References

1. HART, W. O. and GARNER, J. F., *Hart's Introduction to the Law of Local Government and Administration* (Butterworth, 1973).
2. JACKSON, P. W., *Local Government* (Butterworth, 1976).
3. SEELEY, I. H., *Planned Expansion of Country Towns* (George Godwin, 1974).
4. STUDY GROUP ON LOCAL AUTHORITY MANAGEMENT STRUCTURES, *The New Local Authorities: Management and Structure* – the Bains Report (H.M.S.O., 1972).
5. JONES, G. W., 'The Functions and Organisation of Councillors', *Public Administration*, 51 (1973).
6. JACKSON, W. E., *The Structure of Local Government in England and Wales* (Longman, 1966).
7. *Report of the Committee on the Management of Local Government* – the Maud Report (H.M.S.O., 1967).
8. KNOWLES, R. S. B., *Modern Management in Local Government* (Butterworth, 1971).
9. WARREN, J. H., *Municipal Administration* (Pitman, 1954).
10. MALLABY, G., *Local Government Councillors – Their Motives and Manners* (Barry Rose Publications, 1976).
11. GRUGEON, J., 'Officer-member relationships', *Local Government Chronicle*, 26 November 1976.
12. JONES, G. W., 'How to stay clean', *Local Government Chronicle*, 24 September 1976.

CHAPTER FIVE

MANAGEMENT STRUCTURES AND TECHNIQUES

The Concept of Corporate Management

Corporate management has been an important ingredient of recent local government reports (Maud[1], Bains[2] and Paterson[3]) and has aroused considerable interest among members and officers alike. It aims to provide a framework whereby the needs of a community are viewed comprehensively and the activities of the local authority are planned and directed in a unified manner to satisfy those needs to the fullest extent possible within available resources. The achievement of these aims necessitated considerable restructuring of the internal organisations of local authorities in 1974.

The traditional decision-making process in local government has been structured around committees and the implementation of those decisions by administrative units or departments. Committees prepared budgets and tended to become contestants for their share of the total available resources. The principal authorities (county and district councils) provide a wide range of functions and services which interact and are interdependent one upon another. It is unrealistic to consider individual services in isolation and a corporate approach to the direction and control of a range of interwoven activities should, in theory at least, provide an effective solution.

Knowles[4] has described how the focal point for decision and control at member level could be a management board as advocated by Maud or a policy committee of the type envisaged by Bains. At officer level a strong case was made in 1974 for the merging of some departments under a smaller number of chief officers who together could form a management team under the direction of the chief executive. A unified approach should, it is argued, produce greater efficiency and economy and assist in the co-ordination of functions, services and policies which are all interrelated.

Skitt[5] believes that corporate planning, an important part of corporate management, is not merely concerned with managerial arrangements for the governance of local authority areas. He argues that it is primarily concerned with achieving unity of purpose in local authority affairs to enable a local authority to govern effectively, respond to the needs and aspirations of the electorate and through planning to take account of changing circumstances.

Many local authority activities are interrelated and call for comprehensive planning and control. Buchanan[6] showed clearly the close relationship of transport and the living environment. Plowden[7] identified the interdependence of children's achievements in primary schools with their family and social environment, while Seebohm[8] showed the interaction of housing, education and social services. Hence corporate management in its widest sense embraces corporate planning and central policy-making, and requires that departmental policies must be formulated within the framework of a master plan incorporating all local authority functions.

The following are main steps in the process of corporate management.

1. To identify and as far as is practicable analyse and quantify the needs and problems of the community.
2. To specify the objectives of the authority and to identify the alternative methods of achieving them.
3. To evaluate these methods and in the light of the resources needed and benefits to be secured decide on appropriate courses of action.
4. To examine the interrelationships of different departments.
5. To formulate action programmes to achieve agreed objectives for several years ahead.
6. To implement action programmes and undertake periodic systematic reviews of programmes and progress.
7. To monitor changing needs and modify action programmes, where necessary, and to evaluate performance.

Thus corporate management constitutes a total system of management embracing planning the activities, undertaking and controlling them, and monitoring and modifying them in the light of experience, all within a concerted or corporate framework.

Background to Corporate Management

Maud Report

The Maud Report[1] criticised the continuance of the nineteenth-century local government arrangements in the mid-twentieth century, whereby members concerned themselves with details of day-to-day administration, much of which could be entrusted to officers. The larger local authorities operated an elaborate system of committees and sub-committees, which the Maud Committee considered ill-suited to deal with the wide range of business, needing as it did co-ordinated long-term action. The work was fragmented between too many separate departments, which were seldom coherently organised. This often resulted in members being so engrossed in detail that little time remained for making important decisions, while officers were unable to develop fully their initiative and expertise.

Central government appeared to be increasingly losing confidence in the responsibility of local authorities, resulting in an excess of central government control, while the local authorities were failing to attract people of the required calibre, either as members or officers, and this deficiency was also highlighted in the Mallaby Report.[9] The Committee also identified a wide gulf in local government between the elected members and the electorate.

The Maud Committee recommended a small number of committees each concerned with groups of services, and that their function should normally cease to be executive or administrative. The Committee proposed the establishment of a management board of five to nine members with wide delegated powers and providing the channel for the passage of committee business to council. The management board would thus become the focal point in the management of a local authority's affairs, and this proved unacceptable to the local authorities who preferred a finance or policy committee with other committees retaining their executive powers. The report also contained recommendations for reformed relationships between central and local government and closer relations between council and public, and these are considered in Chapters 9 and 10.

Bains Report

The Bains Study Group[2] established a number of important principles upon which its recommendations on management structures were based.

1. There is a need for a clear understanding by members and officers of their respective roles in order to secure an effective partnership.
2. All members should satisfactorily fulfil their particular aims and interests and exercise their constituency roles. (The first objective could be questioned as personal interests of members ought to be subordinate to the effective operation of the authority.)
3. There should be adequate monitoring of activities and review of performance.
4. Effective decision-making requires logical delegation so that decisions are made at the lowest practicable level.
5. The traditional departmental approach to management should be replaced by a corporate approach to ensure the most effective use of resources.

6. A policy and resources committee should be established concerned with the formulation and execution of an overall plan, the
setting of objectives and priorities, and the monitoring and review
of performance.
7. A chief executive should be appointed as head of the paid officers,
leading a team of chief officers with a co-ordinating and controlling role.
8. There is a need for a greater awareness of the importance of
personnel management in local government.

The Study Group recognised that local government is not confined
to the provision of services and that its responsibilities extend to
the overall economic, cultural and physical well-being of the
community. On working arrangements, the Study Group favoured
full availability of information to all members, whether of majority
or minority parties. The formulation of policy ought not to be
confined to a central policy committee and policy should be subject
to continuous review. The need for an effective overall plan for
an authority was reaffirmed, together with the establishment of
priorities, monitoring of performance and assessment of effectiveness
of activities. Chief officers should be given adequate authority and
responsibility, and should also advise members in their decision-
making role.

It was believed that a council, in addition to operating as a
decision-making body, should also engage in debate and policy-
formulation. The council should receive co-ordinated advice from
a policy and resources committee, which in its turn should be
supported by four sub-committees to exercise day to day control
over staff, finance, land, and performance review.

The Study Group also recommended the appointment of a chief
executive free of specific departmental responsibilities and the
establishment of a management team of principal chief officers. These
two important aspects will be considered in more detail later in
this chapter.

New Committee Structures

Reasons for Change

The committee system as it had developed prior to local government
reorganisation in 1974 had attempted to combine both policy and
administrative functions. Furthermore, the committees were largely
structured around specific functions or services and this encouraged
a departmental rather than a corporate approach. Some rationalisa-

tion of the multiple committee structure was needed to secure effective co-ordination and the implementation of a unified policy.

New Committee Arrangements

The recommendation of the Maud Committee[1] for a reduction in the number of committees was generally implemented in 1974. This has usually been achieved by a grouping of compatible services and functions, such as the establishment of a leisure, recreation and amenities committee which in a non-metropolitan county might embrace libraries, museums, art galleries, entertainment, country parks, footpaths and bridleways, commons, caravan sites, recreation and tourism. Another approach to grouping is on programme areas, related to services viewed by the consumer – for example, a public protection committee might include police, fire service and consumer protection activities.

In practice the number of service or programme committees varies with local need and some additional to Bain's recommendations have been created – for example, national parks and employment committees. Planning and transportation have often been separated.[10]

The Bains Study Group[2] suggested that a committee structure should provide each member with a seat on at least one committee. In practice many provide two or three seats, and this has become quite an important factor in deciding the number and size of committees. Suffolk decided that a councillor might reasonably expect to serve on one principal committee, two other sub-committees and possibly an outside or joint body.[10]

Some non-metropolitan counties have omitted an amenities and countryside committee as suggested by Bains and few appointed county recreation officers. In 1973 a select committee on sport and leisure of the House of Lords recommended that every county council and metropolitan district council should establish a recreation committee and a recreation department under its own chief officer, and that a statutory duty should be laid on local authorities to provide adequate recreational facilities.

The reduced number of committee seats for members creates the need for effective transmission of information to keep members well informed. Some new authorities have recognised this by adopting the Bains recommendation of making committee agendas available to all members and permitting members to attend and, at the chairman's discretion, speak at meetings of every committee. Many counties have also recognised the need for close co-ordination with district councils and the new water and health authorities through county joint committees.[10]

Policy and Resources Committee

The Bains Report[2] recommended strongly that principal councils should each establish a policy and resources committee to assist in formulating and executing an overall plan for the community. It was believed that such a committee would aid an authority in setting objectives and priorities, co-ordinating and controlling the implementation of those objectives, and monitoring and reviewing performance.

The Paterson Report[3] dealing with Scottish management structures in 1973 prescribed the following far-reaching duties for a policy and resources committee, aimed at fulfilling its overview and corporate role.

1. To guide the council in the formulation of its policy objectives and priorities, including the preparation of forward programmes. To consider the broad social and economic needs of the authority and matters of great importance to the area, including the contents of structure and local plans, and to advise the council on financial and economic policies.
2. Without prejudice to service committees, to review the effectiveness of the council's work and the standards and levels of service provided. To identify the need for new services and to keep existing ones under review.
3. To submit to the council concurrent reports with service committees upon new policies or changes in policy proposed by such committees, particularly where these have significant impact upon the policy plan or resources of the council.
4. To advise the council on the allocation and control of its financial, manpower and land resources.
5. To ensure that the organisation and management processes of the council make the most effective contribution to achieving the council's objectives. To keep them under review in the light of changing circumstances and make such recommendations as the committee thinks fit.
6. To be involved with other appropriate committees in the appointment of heads of departments and deputies.

The establishment of a policy and resources committee is likely to create problems in its relationship with service committees. It is vital that service committees retain responsibility for formulating and implementing policy within their own particular spheres of influence, while the policy and resources committee should be able to review the performance of other committees set against the council's agreed aims and objectives and to submit reports thereon to the council. The service or programme committees should ideally not be subordinate to the policy and resources committee and should have the same right of direct access to the council.

The new non-metropolitan counties saw the need to establish policy and resources committees in 1974, to secure integrated direction and control of local authority affairs. Stewart[11] questioned their validity for metropolitan counties, where he considered, with some justification, that a planning and policy committee should be the central committee, as the policies of these counties mainly centre around planning functions.

Views have differed as to whether or not the opposition party should be represented on the policy and resources committee. The Bains Committee[2] favoured minority-party representation, believing that these members should receive all information made available to the committee and should be able to express their views at this important stage. The Committee also felt that the policy and resources committee should not be composed entirely of committee chairmen. Others have expressed the opposite view in that the function of the committee is to provide a forum where members of the majority party can discuss frankly alternative policies without the inhibiting influence of opposition members. Service or programme committees contain members from all parties and thus ensure full and free debate. It is further argued, with considerable support, that committees with members from two or more parties generally become political debating chambers and, in these circumstances, main policy issues are likely to be decided beforehand in secret party meetings without officer advice, hence it is better to face up to this possibility and man the policy and resources committee entirely with majority-party members.

The Bains Committee[2] proposals for a non-metropolitan county committee structure are illustrated in Figure 5. The diagram shows the policy and resources committee supported by three resource sub-committees dealing with finance, personnel and land, and a fourth sub-committee concerned with performance review. Six service or programme committees cover the main services and functions of a county council.

The finance sub-committee would have responsibility for day-to-day financial matters, the personnel sub-committee for establishment and personnel activities, and the land sub-committee for matters of land and building acquisition, use and disposal. The performance review sub-committee would monitor results against objectives and evaluate standards, and could refer both to programme committees and to officers for information.

The policy and resources committee is primarily concerned with

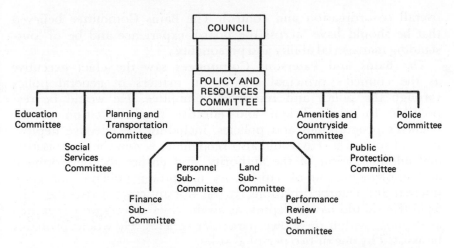

FIGURE 5   *Committee structure – non-metropolitan county (Bains Committee proposals)*

the overall allocation of resources in line with agreed priorities. The resource sub-committees have a continuing function in the detailed allocation and management of a specific resource element, be it finance, personnel or land. The need for resource sub-committees has not been as clearly identifiable by the new authorities and a variety of arrangements operated in 1974. The majority of county councils omitted the performance review sub-committee from their new structures usually on the grounds that time was needed to assess the needs and policies or that some less formal and more sensitive mechanism might be devised.[10]

Chief Executive

Both the Maud[1] and Mallaby[9] Reports in 1967 saw the role of the clerk of the council as chief executive in the suggested reformed structure for local authorities. The Maud Report envisaged the chief executive as a team leader and co-ordinator, and as a focal point for unified direction at officer level.

The Bains Report[2] in 1972 supported the recommendation of the Maud Committee for one person to be designated as the head of the authority's paid service with authority over the other chief officers to secure efficient and effective management and execution of the authority's functions. Hence the role of the chief executive was intended to be very different to that of the traditional clerk – free of all departmental responsibilities, head of the paid service and leader of a small management team of chief officers, to secure overall co-ordination and control. The Bains Committee believed that he should have 'across the board' experience and be of 'outstanding managerial ability and personality'.

The Bains and Paterson[3] Committees saw the chief executive as the council's principal adviser on matters of general policy through the policy and resources committee. He would be responsible for the efficient and effective implementation of the council's programmes and policies, including the effective deployment of resources. He would also keep under review the organisation and administration of the authority, and ensure the development and implementation of satisfactory manpower policies and good internal and external relations. It was not anticipated that the chief executive should have a deputy, as all the chief officers were regarded as deputies within their own particular spheres. He would probably be assisted by one or two personal aides.

Figure 6 illustrates the proposed Bains departmental structure for one of the larger non-metropolitan districts.

Bains[12] has described the advantages accruing to heads of other departments through regular direct access to an uncommitted chief executive. He believed that chief executives would be kept well apprised through regular meetings with their management teams, members, other local authorities and government departments, and would certainly not be out of touch. As in industry the measure of success of a chief executive is likely to be proportional to the extent to which he influences others. His own work is often of limited

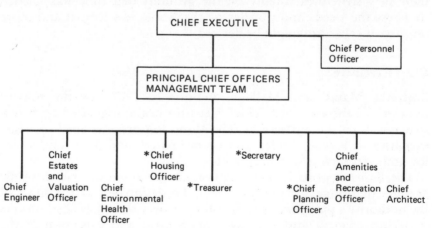

* Members of management team. Local circumstances
may justify additional members.

FIGURE 6   *Departmental structure – larger non-metropolitan district (Bains Committee proposals)*

consequence compared with what he can accomplish through constructive influence on others.

Greenwell[13] has described how the chief executive must aim at creating a climate of opinion among members and officers favourable to the corporate process. He is the recipient of a large volume of information from the public, members and officers, and against this background knowledge he weighs competing claims for resources and, in close consultation with the treasurer, tenders advice to the council on the allocation of resources. The chief executive stands as a bridge between chief officers and members. He must enjoy the confidence of members, to produce a satisfactory strategy based on their broad objectives, and be trusted by chief officers to obtain fair treatment for their services and, on occasions, to act as friend at court. The chief executive also has to secure a fair allocation of government resources for his authority.

Greenwell[13] has shown how a chief executive must be aware of the aims and priorities of the majority party and understand the pressures to which the leader is subjected in maintaining his position and authority within the group. He must achieve a rapport with the leader but not become so closely involved as to be regarded as personally committed to the policies of the majority party. The chief executive should also be available to the leader of the opposition displaying complete impartiality and the utmost discretion.

Management Team

The management team envisaged in the Bains Report[2] comprises the chief executive and a group of chief officers, and has been likened to the officer counterpart of the policy and resources committee. The Study Group felt that the management team should number about six and so some of the chief officers in a larger authority might not be members. In practice varying sizes of team are operating – for example, Suffolk's team initially contained eleven members and it was argued that a smaller team would militate against a true corporate spirit and that on few occasions only would all members be present.[10]

The management team is essentially a working party of chief officers providing a focal point for the preparation of co-ordinated advice on policies and major programmes of work for presentation to the council through the policy and resources committee. All members are committed to act with the wider objectives of the authority in mind, and not as individual chief officers concerned solely with the activities and interests of their own departments.

In this way a wide range of skills, expertise and knowledge can be welded together in a corporate approach for the benefit of the authority as a whole.

The Bains Report[2] recognised that few, if any, major decisions can be made in isolation without some impact upon others' areas of responsibility. Corporate management requires that the implications for the authority as a whole should be considered before decisions are taken. On occasions chief officers will be obliged to subordinate their own interests to that of the authority.

The Bains Committee identified two broad functions for the management team: the preparation of plans and programmes relating to the long-term strategy of the authority and the overall checking of progress and implementation. The Committee also believed that the chief executive and management team should establish a system of inter-disciplinary working groups to serve programme committees, with each group under the control of a senior officer from a discipline appropriate to the group.

Greenwell[13] has described how a management team brings together a wide cross-section of attitudes and professional backgrounds, and how some members are interested primarily in their own departments and may feel inhibited in offering advice on wider issues; others endeavour to protect their resources against all-comers, while some with no service commitment, such as the treasurer, secretary and architect, will express their views more freely. Greenwell believes that prospects for effective management-team working are improving as individual chief officers recognise that they are dependent upon each other's understanding and support for the successful implementation of council policies which they have helped to formulate, and are less inclined to use the meetings for airing grievances.

In the view of Miller,[14] a county treasurer, corporate management needs more than a structure – it needs a certain attitude of mind. It is probable that every chief officer and every chairman who assists in the corporate management of an authority is doing a better job than he would do on his own, but he is, nevertheless, surrendering a little of his personal power and responsibility in the interests of the common good.

Corporate Management in Action

New Local Authority Structures

On 1 April 1974 the new local authorities with their revised management structures commenced activities in England and Wales. Each council had a central policy committee on the lines suggested by the Bains Committee[2] or one modified according to local choice. The emphasis varied between authorities from co-ordination to policy-making and control. The size of the central policy committee varied from ten to 45 members,[15] with few adopting single-party membership of this important committee. In some authorities sub-committees of the central policy committee were created for finance, personnel, land and performance reviews, while in others the functions of finance and personnel continued to be administered by main committees. The majority of authorities reduced the number of committees.

Every new authority, except Derby District Council, appointed a chief executive officer as head of the paid service and in the majority of authorities he was freed of departmental duties, although in some authorities he still had responsibility for the operation of a service, usually legal or administrative. The counties showed a small reduction in the number of chief officers.[16]

All new authorities have created management teams but these show considerable diversity in the number of chief officers in the teams (three to twelve) and the services they represent.[17] Some authorities have followed the Bains Committee recommendation for the abolition of standing deputy chief officers, but others have adhered to the former arrangement. A considerable number of specialist technical officers have been appointed to cover specific aspects of planning or management. The majority of district councils set up six departments finance, administration, public health, housing, technical services and planning. The technical services committee usually embraces engineering, estates, architectural services and direct labour work.[17]

County Council Structures

Hender[18] believes that the corporate management approach must be related to the particular needs, traditions and circumstances of the authority. Those contributing must understand what is expected of them, how they fit in with other parts of the organisation and how their contribution assists in producing positive results. He also sees the need for an annual review process to take account of changing economic, social and physical factors, and he sees benefits accruing to the following sectors from corporate planning.

1. *The public* gain a deeper understanding of the issues involved, and receive improved information and greater benefit from use of public resources.

2. *Members* gain from deeper understanding and probing of vital issues and from the sense of unity, and they are better able to influence major decisions.
3. *Officers* benefit from the generation of team spirit and are able to express views and have them considered before decisions are made.

Greenwell[19] has described how Northamptonshire County Council rearranged council and committee meetings on a quarterly cycle, except the planning and transportation committee, which meets on a six-weekly cycle. Standing sub-committees are to be avoided wherever possible and there is substantial delegation to chief officers. Greenwell[19] believes that the selection of chief officers for the management team should be based on the contribution that the officers have to make rather than their being the holders of specific posts, and once appointed to the management team they require assistance from a senior officer in the day-to-day management of their departments.

Smith[20] has described how Suffolk County Council aimed to achieve an open and relaxed style of local government. He sees the advantage of a chief executive with no departmental responsibilities as having time to see the complete picture, and pursue an outward-looking role, to discuss chief officers' problems and help members through the complexities of the organisation illustrated in Figure 7. Suffolk's aim is 'to inform and be informed'. Hence chief officers are free to attend any committee meetings.

The Suffolk policy and resources committee comprises 21 members, drawn in strict proportion from the political groups. A performance review sub-committee was established with the following priorities.

1. Review of the working of the management structure.
2. Examination of relationships with bodies such as health and water authorities and statutory undertakings (subsequently deferred).
3. Examination of effectiveness of agency arrangements.
4. Review of effect of continuing different standards in the areas of old authorities.

The sub-committee has also conducted a joint review with a district council and other relevant bodies to look at the use of all public land and buildings in a specific area with a view to improving facilities and reducing costs.

Suffolk County Council is also pursuing other Bains Committee[2] recommendations, such as joint working groups of members and

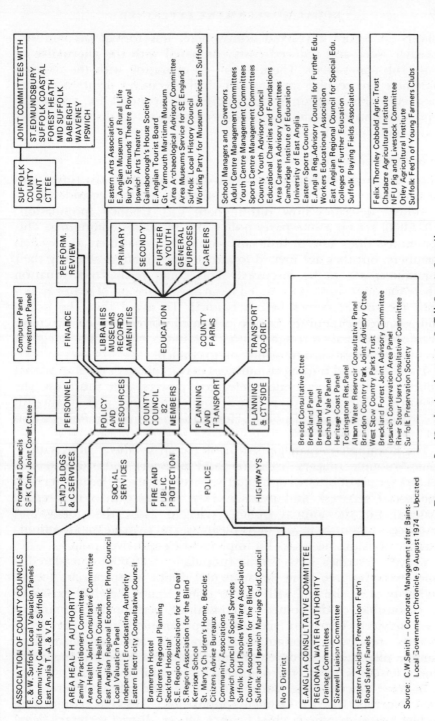

FIGURE 7 *Member involvement – Suffolk County Council*

Source: C.W.Smith – Corporate Management after Bains:
Local Government Chronicle, 9 August 1974 – Updated

officers to secure a relaxed atmosphere, less formal preparation, speedier work and reduced costs compared with the alternative of more sub-committees. There is full co-operation with the districts and there are regular meetings of chief executives prior to county joint committee meetings. An interesting proposal for reciprocal representation of membership between county and district councils is also under consideration.

District Council Structures

There are wide variations between district council structures, and some aspects of three very different authorities are now considered.

Amos[21] describes how Birmingham City Council (population: 1 087 000) set up a one-party policy and resources committee. This committee does not include any committee chairmen as ex-officio members, but they are invited to attend when matters affecting their committees are to be discussed. This could result in a situation where the opposition is excluded from any discussion of major policy until the matter comes before council. To avoid this, the policy and resources committee has no delegated powers and all executive decisions must pass through another committee either for a delegated decision or for onward transmission to council.

The service and trading committees may implement their approved policies and budgets under delegated powers, but must use the resources committees to procure land, personnel and finance in accordance with overall policy. Hence the resource committees also act in a co-ordinative role.

The Birmingham management team comprises the chief executive, some resource officers (treasurer and planner) and some service officers (education, environmental services, housing, leisure services and social services), and meets weekly. Its function is to prepare material for the annual policy cycle, to assist the policy and resources committee in any of its business, and to make major administrative decisions necessary for implementing approved policy.

Keast[22] describes how Pendle (population: 86 000) considered a chief executive free from departmental duties inappropriate for an authority of its size and with its functions. Hence the chief executive is responsible for the control of committee, personnel and management services. There are six other departments which, apart from finance, represent groupings of functions and responsibilities, namely planning and development, combined technical engineer/ works, leisure services, environmental health, and housing.

Bolton[23] describes the management team and officer structure for West Norfolk District Council (population: 115 000), comprising a chief executive officer, chief finance officer, district secretary (legal and administrative support services), chief personnel and management services adviser (personnel and management services; computer), chief development officer (engineering, planning and architectural services; industrial development), chief environmental health officer (general environmental health services; housing policy advice), and three area managers (management of services in each area of the authority). Subsequently this authority faced overmanning problems.

The Application of Corporate Management

Thornhill[24] has highlighted some of the difficulties that arise in applying corporate management to local government. They stem mainly from the sharing of management functions between members and officers, the wide variation in size of authorities and the different ways in which local authorities have organised themselves.

Some of the management structures adopted by local authorities retain the traditional council, committee and officer relationship, which may make the implementation of effective corporate management very difficult. The ingrained departmental approach can constitute a serious obstacle, and Thornhill[25] suggests that this problem might re-emerge through past traditions of longer-serving members and the forging of links between programme committees and groups of officers.

Where a policy and resources or management committee is composed mainly of committee chairmen, it will be difficult for them to shed their representative capacities and act in an objective, impartial role at the central level.[24] The all-party approach to membership of the central committee is feared by some to lead to a weakening of corporate management through political compromise, despite its democratic appeal.

Surveys of post-1974 local authority management systems show that many committees are being retained with executive responsibilities, even though the committees are generally fewer in number with a broader range of activities. The majority of management teams comprise executive heads of departments. Both of these arrangements are likely to weaken the implementation of corporate management, and there is a danger that the central committee may be reduced to a co-ordinating vehicle rather than a management one.[26]

The management teams are generally of a larger size than advocated by Bains and consist mainly of chief officers. It will take time to combat the entrenched departmental approach of many chief officers and divert to other interests those members who wish to exercise a direct influence over particular activities.[26]

Management Techniques

Management Services

The Maud Report[1] recommended that local authorities should adopt 'a systematic approach to the processes of management'. Since 1974 an increasing number of chief executives have taken overall charge of personnel management (described in Chapter 6) and management services, which include such techniques as work study, organisation and methods, operational research, network analysis, cost–benefit analysis and the use of computers. Local authorities, particularly the larger ones, have been prominent in using management aids or tools and in exploiting the potential of the computer.

Knowles[4] has defined two broad categories of management services – those that assist the decision-making process, and those that seek to promote operational efficiency. They are essentially advisory in character and need to be operated with skill and understanding. Prior to the investigation of a service, preliminary discussions should take place between the departmental head and management services officer to agree the terms of reference, method of operation and other related matters. Considerable care and skill is also required in the drafting of reports, aiming at clarity and brevity, emphasising possible improvements, not overemphasising present deficiencies and finishing with a summary which is concise and easily understood.

The Bains Report[2] describes management services as 'all services which help management to plan, control and improve the activities of the organisation in a general sense'. The Study Group considered that management services could validly reside in various parts of an authority's organisation, and did not necessarily require to be administered within a single monolithic management services unit. Some techniques may be most effectively implemented by placing them within individual departments though others will, by their nature, require to be centrally administered. Indeed, the Study Group received considerable conflicting evidence on the grouping and operation of management services. With larger authorities there is likely to be a need for a central research and intelligence unit to obtain, analyse and circulate information throughout the authority.

Employment of Private Consultants

Since the early 1950s many local authorities have engaged private consultants to advise on management matters or to provide specialist services. On occasions private consultants with a commercial and industrial background have been confused by the local government structure with its democratic control, management by committees and central government oversight. In their turn authorities have not always been satisfied with the consultants, whose not inconsiderable fees will be largely abortive if the recommendations are not implemented. Sometimes authorities are disenchanted with the consultants' recommendations and on a reappraisal feel that the investigation could have been carried out equally effectively by their own staff at much less cost. There is often understandable opposition from officers to the engagement of private consultants.

Knowles[4] has identified four basic criteria to be applied by authorities contemplating engaging private consultants.

1. Clear definition of the service to be provided.
2. Careful selection of the consultant.
3. Clearly defined terms of reference agreed with the consultant.
4. Close working arrangements with the consultant throughout the assignment.

Local authorities should ideally hold preliminary discussions with representatives of each of the short-listed organisations, followed possibly by further discussions in depth with one or two consultants, selected from the short-list, to identify objectives and possible achievements based on past experience. A selected consultant usually quotes a fee for making a survey and preparing a feasibility study, which will identify the limits of the investigation, the improvements that can reasonably be expected and the cost and duration of the assignment. The authority does not commit itself to the investigation until it has considered and approved the feasibility study.

LAMSAC

LAMSAC (the Local Authorities Management Services and Computer Committee) was established in 1967 and comprises members and officers from its constituent bodies. Its broad objectives are the co-ordination of research, development and training, and the establishment of a central library of information and clearing house for the benefit of local authorities. It liaises with governmental and other bodies and advises local authorities on the latest and most effective methods.

Planning, Programming and Budgeting Systems

These arrangements, commonly described as P.P.B.S. have been defined as 'a system for analysing programmed expenditure by reference to particular objectives, instead of under input headings such as staff, buildings and equipment'.[27] The main characteristics are as follows.

1. To identify the objectives which the organisation is attempting to achieve and to express them in quantifiable terms.
2. To secure the effectiveness of an activity or group of activities in meeting the agreed objectives.
3. To prepare a programme budget forecasting the outputs and expenditures for a period of, say, five years.
4. To review annually the achieved outputs and expenditures.
5. To analyse alternative policies to achieve objectives in the light of changing conditions.

In the search for greater efficiency, some authorities are introducing *management by objectives*, which has been defined as 'a technique under which targets are fixed as a basis for achieving greater effectiveness throughout the whole of an organisation or part of it'.[27] It aims to create a framework for the improved working of departments and sections. It is therefore distinguishable from P.P.B.S., concerned with corporate planning throughout the authority, but can be successfully integrated into it.

Management by objectives generally involves the determination of key tasks and work targets for individual officers. On closer examination an officer will often find that some of his duties are non-key tasks in that they do not contribute to the achievement of his objectives and, if they are still necessary, he should endeavour to have them performed elsewhere. The officer should carry out a regular review of performance against targets. This approach aims to secure an organisational structure which gives a chief officer maximum freedom and flexibility of action, coupled with effective central management control and information transmission to permit quick and effective decision-making.[28]

Anthony[29] suggests that there are three main management processes in a continuing cycle in most larger organisations, and these have their applications to local government. Figure 8 illustrates these processes.

Work Study

Work study is defined by the British Standards Institution in B.S. 3138:599 as 'a generic term for those techniques, particularly method study and work measurement, which are used in the examination of human work in all its contexts and which lead systematically to the investigation of all the factors which affect the efficiency and economy of the situation being reviewed, in order to effect improvement'. This technique has been widely used in local government to improve productivity, principally with outdoor services. It is based on detailed observation and careful measurement and so provides

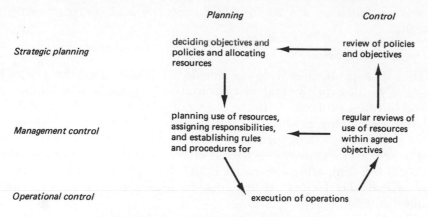

Planning   *Control*

Strategic planning   deciding objectives and   review of policies
                            policies and allocating   and objectives
                            resources

Management control   planning use of resources,   regular reviews of
                            assigning responsibilities,   use of resources
                            and establishing rules   within agreed
                            and procedures for   objectives

Operational control   execution of operations

FIGURE 8   *Main management processes cycle*

a sound basis for incentive bonus schemes. The author has listed the criteria to be observed in formulating incentive schemes[30] and their application to refuse collection, housing maintenance and other local authority services[31] as a means of increasing productivity and reducing operating costs while at the same time maintaining the quality of the service.

The Bains Study Group[2] recommended that most work study officers should operate within individual departments, although there could still be a need for a small central unit to control overall deployment of work study staff and ensure that new techniques are evaluated and staff trained in their use.

Organisation and Methods

This technique has been defined as 'a service giving advice on the structure of an organisation, its management and control, and its procedure and methods'.[27] It is often applied to administrative arrangements to secure more efficient and economical methods, often by simplifying procedures which enable professionals to devote more time to their professional work and less on purely clerical activities. It could also deal with wider issues such as whether architectural, quantity surveying and planning staff should form part of a department of technical services or whether they should constitute separate departments. The investigation is normally undertaken by an O. and M. team or unit that examines and analyses present arrangements and makes such proposals as it considers appropriate. The Bains Study Group[2] believed that the O. and M. unit should be under the wing of head of administration, but should be very much an aid to the chief executive and the management team.

Operational Research

This is a problem-solving technique in which scientific research – analytical, experimental or quantitative – is applied to industrial and business problems with the object of providing a more analytical basis for making predictions and decisions.[27] A common approach to a decision-making problem where there is risk of uncertainty is to seek to measure the factors of chance and to develop a scientific model for comparing alternative courses of action. Its greatest value is where the factors under consideration are complicated and intertwined.[4]

The Local Government Operational Research Unit uses operational research techniques to assist local authorities in their policy and management decisions, covering a wide range of activities from ordering procedures to housing maintenance.[32] The Unit publishes the results of its studies, provides assistance to authorities that wish to implement them and co-operates with other research bodies.

Network Analysis

This technique comprises preparing a plan of action using an arrow diagram or network, which clearly depicts the various actions which are needed to complete a project and their interrelationship. The optimum combination will normally represent the lowest cost, subject to availability of resources, and this can be determined by network analysis. Certain of the operations are critical, in that if they are delayed or prolonged the completion of the job will also be delayed. Network analysis pinpoints the critical operations and enables the time leeway for all other operations to be determined.[31] This technique assists in the programming of work and in the economic deployment of resources.

There are three main approaches.

1. Critical path analysis (C.P.A.), in which establishing the critical route identifies those parts of the job requiring most attention.
2. Programme evaluation and review technique (PERT) progressively establishes new critical routes as conditions change.
3. Resource allocation and multi-project scheduling (RAMPS) interjects conflicting criteria, such as cost versus time, into the determination of the optimum routes.

Cost–benefit Analysis

Cost–benefit analysis has been defined as 'a technique of use in either investment appraisal or the review of the operation of a service for analysing and measuring the costs and benefits to the community of adopting specified courses of action and for examining the incidence of these costs and benefits between different sections of the community'.[33] It has the basic objective of identifying and measuring the costs and benefits which stem from either the investment of monies or the operation of a service, but in particular it is concerned with examining not only those costs and benefits which have a direct impact on the providing authority but also those which are of an external nature and accrue to other persons. Furthermore, the costs and benefits to be measured are those which accrue throughout the life of the project.

Problems arise in determining cut-off points for the exclusion of remote factors and in quantifying, yet alone evaluating, some of the more intangible items. The value attached to non-working time became the dominant factor in the M1 and Victoria Line studies, and the author has illustrated the practical difficulties of applying the technique to the evaluation of outdoor recreational facilities.[34]

Use of Computers

The computer has had a revolutionary affect on many aspects of local government administration because of its great potential. The main benefits stem from its ability to handle data with accuracy, the remarkable speed of operation, the storage and retrieval of masses of information using very little space and the solving of infinitely complex problems. Its uses embrace record-keeping, including payroll and inventory accounting, provision of management information systems, information storage and retrieval, and model simulation and design aids.

Computers are generally contained within treasurers' departments because of the financial and payroll tasks undertaken. The Bains Study Group[2] saw merit in the control of computer time and facilities being vested in a separate body responsible direct to the management team.

Departmental Organisation

Departmental Structures

The internal organisation of local authorities in the United Kingdom has largely evolved around departments, each organised under the administrative direction of a chief officer. Each department is responsible for performing certain specified services and functions of the authority. Some are service departments providing major local authority services such as housing, public health, education and social services, although these will vary with the type of authority, its functions and organisation. Other departments provide a supporting role to the service departments and these include legal, finance, personnel and supplies departments.

Departmentalism stemmed from the statutory requirements to appoint certain officers and because the larger authorities needed groups of professional officers, which tended to be organised in departments under a senior officer of the same discipline. Thus the requirement to appoint a chief education officer led logically to the formation of an education department under his direction, responsible for the administration of the authority's educational functions. Architects' departments became established in most counties concerned with the provision of new buildings and often the maintenance and alteration of existing ones, and included officers of other disciplines besides architects who were involved in the building process, such as quantity surveyors, structural engineers, heating engineers and clerks of works.

Many local authority departments are accordingly headed by officers with specific professional qualifications and with extensive practical experience in this particular sphere. Much of the time of chief officers is spent on managerial matters in which few of them receive any initial training. Nevertheless, Bains[2] recommended that the officer structure of the new local authorities should be founded upon the existing professional base, not least because the best potential managers in the short and medium term are to be found already established in the professions of local government.

Prior to 1974 departmental chief officers were rarely answerable to the senior chief officer, but usually to the clerk. This fragmented departmental structure was criticised by both Maud[1] and Bains.[2] Doubtless co-ordination of activities and policies could be difficult without considerable understanding and co-operation from the departmental heads.

Maud and Bains both advocated reducing the number of departments by suitable groupings, and this was achieved by many authorities in 1974. For example, Nottingham City Council combined the former architect's, engineer's and estates departments into a single integrated department of technical services, and Nottinghamshire County Council combined the highways and planning departments, recognising the close interrelationship of these two functions.

The Bains Study Group recommended that the departmental structure should continue to be based upon the services required by the authority in order to fulfil its plans and objectives. Although it strongly advocated the breaking of the one-department-one-committee link to promote the development of a corporate approach to management. The Study Group recognised the substantial problems in grouping departments together under directors, particularly if the directors were merely to exercise a co-ordinating role. There is no real justification for putting efficiently run departments into illogical groupings merely to secure an even workload between directors.

In some cases the committee and departmental structure will no longer coincide and some other organisation will be needed, such as inter-disciplinary working groups to serve programme committees. In addition area offices, operating under clearly defined delegated powers, will be required in the larger authorities.[2]

Larger departments are often subdivided into sections. For instance, a finance department might be grouped under accountancy, audit, income, salaries and superannuation, and computer and data processing sections. In other departments, such as education and highways, there may be a system of divisional or district officers.

Role of Chief Officers

Many chief officers believe their main function to be running a department, rather than achieving objectives. Frequently chief officers are supported by deputies – although their value is now being questioned in some quarters – and these often accept much of the responsibility for day-to-day operation of the department. In these circumstances the chief officer is likely to retain control of certain key issues and matters of special interest, and to devote the major part of his time to policy and planning matters.[4]

A chief officer is responsible for the management and discipline of his department, in addition to giving professional advice. Ideally he should be able to weld his staff into an effective and contented work force, and be able to give the required inspiration through personal example, good working relationships and by keeping the staff informed of important issues. The chief officer will normally wish to see all draft reports for committees, most incoming mail and certain categories of outgoing letters. He will generally need to attend all committee meetings impinging upon his department's work and meetings of chief officers.[4]

Many departments contain a wide range of personnel – professional, technical, administrative and clerical, and sometimes manual operatives in addition. It is essential to foster satisfactory and harmonious working relationships between them to secure a team approach. The important role of section leaders, supervisors and foremen must be recognised and these personnel given the status and backing that they deserve.

References

1. *Report of the Committee on the Management of Local Government* – the Maud Report (H.M.S.O., 1967).
2. STUDY GROUP ON LOCAL AUTHORITY MANAGEMENT STRUCTURES, *The New Local Authorities: Management and Structure* – the Bains Report (H.M.S.O., 1972).
3. *The New Scottish Local Authorities – Organisation and Management Structures* – the Paterson Report (H.M.S.O., 1973).
4. KNOWLES, R. S. B., *Modern Management in Local Government* (Butterworth, 1971).
5. SKITT, J. (ed), *Practical Corporate Planning in Local Government* (Leonard Hill, 1975).
6. MINISTRY OF TRANSPORT, *Traffic in Towns* – the Buchanan Report (H.M.S.O., 1963).
7. *Children and their Primary Schools* – the Plowden Committee Report (H.M.S.O., 1967).
8. Cmnd. 3703, *Report of the Committee on Local Authority and Allied Personal Social Services* (H.M.S.O., 1968).
9. *Report of the Committee on the Staffing of Local Government* – the Mallaby Report (H.M.S.O., 1967).
10. STEWART, J. D., 'Management structures – setting up the new counties', *Municipal and Public Services Journal,* 25 May 1973.
11. STEWART, J. D., 'The Metropolitan Counties', *Municipal and Public Services Journal,* 9 March 1973.
12. BAINS, M., 'Corporate management after Bains', *Local Government Chronicle,* 13 September 1974.
13. GREENWELL, J., 'The true role of the chief executive', *Local Government Chronicle,* 3 September 1976.
14. MILLER, J. V., 'The treasurer and corporate management', *Local Government Chronicle,* 2 August 1974.
15. INSTITUTE OF LOCAL GOVERNMENT STUDIES, *Local government reorganisation – emergent structures* (Birmingham University, 1974).
16. KEAST, H., 'Committee structures in the counties', *Local Government Chronicle,* 23 August 1974.
17. KEAST, H., 'Committee structures in the districts', *Local Government Chronicle,* 13 December 1974.
18. HENDER, J. D., 'Corporate management after Bains', *Local Government Chronicle,* 17 May 1974.
19. GREENWELL, J., 'Corporate management after Bains', *Local Government Chronicle,* 14 June 1974.
20. SMITH, C. W., 'Corporate management after Bains', *Local Government Chronicle,* 9 August 1974.
21. AMOS, F. J. C., 'Corporate management after Bains', *Local Government Chronicle,* 26 July 1974.

22. KEAST, H., 'Reorganisation at Pendle', *Local Government Chronicle*, 15 February 1974.
23. BOLTON, J., 'Corporate management after Bains', *Local Government Chronicle*, 7 June 1974.
24. THORNHILL, W., 'The application of corporate management', *Local Government Chronicle*, 16 August 1974.
25. THORNHILL, W., 'Management in 1974 . . . 1', *Local Government Chronicle*, 7 February 1975.
26. THORNHILL, W., 'Management in 1974 . . . 2', *Local Government Chronicle*, 14 February 1975.
27. H.M. TREASURY, *Glossary of Management Techniques* (H.M.S.O., 1967).
28. HUMBLE, J., *Improving Management Performance* (McGraw-Hill, 1973).
29. ANTHONY, R., *Planning and Control Systems – a Framework for Analysis* (Harvard Business, 1965).
30. SEELEY, I. H., *Building Maintenance* (Macmillan, 1976).
31. SEELEY, I. H., *Municipal Engineering Practice* (Macmillan, 1967).
32. LOCAL GOVERNMENT OPERATIONAL RESEARCH UNIT, Report No C188: *Evaluating Alternative Housing Maintenance Strategies* (H.M.S.O., 1973).
33. HENDER, J. D., 'Introduction to Cost–Benefit Analysis', *Cost–Benefit Analysis* (Institute of Municipal Treasurers and Accountants, 1968).
34. SEELEY, I. H., *Outdoor Recreation and the Urban Environment* (Macmillan, 1973).

CHAPTER SIX

LOCAL GOVERNMENT ADMINISTRATION

Committee Procedures

Standing Orders

The Local Government Act 1972 empowers local authorities to make standing orders regulating the conduct of committee and joint committee meetings and covering the quorum, proceedings and place of meetings. The Ministry has issued model standing orders and these provide guidelines for local authorities in the regulation of council and committee meetings and business.[1]

The Local Government Act 1972 also prescribes that at least three clear days' notice shall be given of all meetings of principal councils (county and district councils), giving the time and place of the intended meeting. The summons to attend the meeting shall specify the business proposed to be transacted.

Standing orders will normally include the following aspects relating to council meetings: frequency, chairman, quorum for a meeting, order of business, notices of motion, motions and amendments which may be moved without notice, questions, minutes, rules of debate, motions affecting persons employed by the council, disorderly conduct of members, disturbance by members of the public, rescission of earlier resolutions, voting, record of attendances, and interests of members or officers in contracts or other matters. Standing orders will also contain procedures relating to committee meetings, such as appointment, proceedings, constitution, election of chairman, special meetings, sub-committees, quorum, voting, and variation, revocation, suspension and interpretation of standing orders. Standing orders often define the terms of reference of committees, the procedure for the presentation of reports, the order of debate, the length of speeches, the form of motions and amendments and the duties of and authority delegated to chief officers.[2]

The form and content of standing orders vary with the constitution and nature of the local authority. Standing orders need to be clear and explicit in their wording and fair and reasonable in their operation. They are of great value to chairmen, members and officers in obtaining uniformity of procedure at meetings, thus avoiding disorder and ensuring the smooth and effective dispatch of business.

The rights of members are thereby safeguarded and abrupt changes in procedure prevented.

Standing orders cannot supplant the law. They can be quite readily created, amended or rescinded by resolution of the council. The adoption of procedures contrary to standing orders, undesirable though it may be, will not usually have any legal consequences.

General Arrangements at Meetings

The Local Government Act 1972 prescribes that all questions shall be decided by a majority of members present and voting at a meeting. The names of the members present shall be recorded. Minutes of the proceedings of meetings shall be prepared and subsequently signed by the chairman. Minutes may be recorded on loose leaves consecutively numbered and duly signed, and each leaf initialled. Minutes are available for inspection by electors, who may make copies or abstracts.

Voting on most issues is by show of hands. There are however occasions when the matters considered are contentious or political views are divided, and in these circumstances the recording of votes is advisable. Members may request that votes be recorded.

The agenda for a committee meeting often consists of correspondence, matters referred to the committee by the council, matters raised by members and reports of officers, while a council meeting will be very much concerned with consideration of committee reports, be they detailed minutes or explanatory reports. Some matters are delegated to the committee for decision, and in these cases the committee will report periodically to the council on the action taken.

Committee proceedings are less formal than those of the full council. Members are able to speak more than once on any item and officers to interject freely to give advice. The chairman usually takes a major part in the discussions, in addition to presiding over the committee, and he will present and speak to the committee's report in the council meeting. In some cases consultation with other interested committees will be needed, and proposals involving the spending of money will be passed to the finance committee.

Public Access to Meetings

The Public Bodies (Admission to Meetings) Act 1960, originating from a private member's bill by Margaret Thatcher, opened council and education committee meetings to the public and the press. The Local Government Act 1972 extended this facility to meetings of all committees, including joint committees. A council or committee may however resolve to exclude the public during consideration of an item where publicity could be prejudicial to the public interest, because of the confidential nature of the matter or for some other special reason.

For instance, items involving the appointment, dismissal or salaries of officers are matters which ought not to be discussed in public. Contentious matters and those where litigation is possible are other examples of items where the public should be excluded from the proceedings. Nevertheless the exclusion of the public and the press from meetings should be exceptional and only operated when absolutely necessary.

Appointment of Committee Members

The council's standing orders will prescribe the method of appointment of committee members and procedures vary between authorities. Members may be nominated by a selection committee for approval by the council; one person may be appointed to each committee representing a parish, ward or other geographical area; membership may be proportional to the relative strengths of the political parties; members may be selected by a balloting process; or some other approach may be adopted. The standing orders often prescribe the minimum and maximum number of committees upon which a member can serve, typical limits being two and six.

Ideally members should be permitted to serve on committees in whose work they have special knowledge or interest. Some committees such as finance, education and planning are generally believed to be more important or interesting than some others, and members are understandably keen to serve on these.

Chairmen of Councils and Committees

The council chairman is appointed at the annual meeting of the authority and must be a member of the authority. He will remain in office until his successor is appointed, unless he resigns or becomes disqualified. His main function is to preside at council meetings but he also represents the council at many business and social functions. A chairman has a casting vote in the event of an equal vote occurring.

New committee chairmen should ideally have considerable local government experience, preferably including that of the committee they are proposing to chair. The procedure for appointment varies between authorities; some committees retain the same chairmen for lengthy periods, some appoint annually, while others appoint for specified periods such as two or three years. The appointment may be made by the committee at its first meeting or by the council. There is an increasing tendency for the majority party to have a predominance of members on all committees and to appoint all committee chairmen at a meeting of party members.

A committee chairman maintains order at committee meetings, decides points of order, ensures that the business is conducted effectively and adjourns the meeting when appropriate. He must ensure that the meeting is properly constituted with eligible persons and that it is quorate. He also has a duty to ensure compliance with standing orders, to see that members have adequate opportunity to express their views, to maintain the scheduled sequence of business unless it is varied by the committee, and to see that the committee's decision is consistent with the information given and members' expressed views. The committee chairman acts as a co-ordinator, guiding free discussion, maintaining order, extricating the general feeling of the committee and helping to frame effective decisions. He ensures that the minutes are properly prepared and, after approval by the committee, signs them.

The committee chairman liaises closely with the head of the department or departments whose work is the concern of the committee. He often requires considerable background information which only the chief officer can provide, and the administrative function is shared between them. On occasions a chairman will need to make a decision in advance of the committee meeting on an urgent matter, and will subsequently seek ratification of his action by the committee. There will probably be some matters which are delegated to the chairman for decision, and for these no subsequent approval is needed.

Programme of Meetings

Committee and council meetings are normally programmed for a year in advance at fixed regular intervals, and the full list of meetings is circulated to all members and appropriate officers. Careful programming of committee meetings is necessary to obtain a satisfactory sequence where the work of one committee impinges on another.

Agenda

The preparation of the list of items to form an agenda is commenced almost immediately after the preceding committee meeting. There are various sources of agenda items.

1. Matters continuing or deferred from previous meeting.

2. Correspondence to be reported to or requiring a decision by the committee.
3. Officers' reports, returns and statistical data.
4. Matters referred by another committee, the council or some other organisation.

Prior to the date for dispatch of the final agenda, a draft is often circulated to interested officers for comment and discussed by the chief officer with the committee chairman. The committee clerk needs to liaise closely with the appropriate officers to ensure that all scheduled reports will be available for dispatch with the agenda.

Agenda are often arranged so that routine non-controversial items receive early consideration. Sufficient information should be included on agenda to identify clearly the items to be discussed and the advance circulation of reports enables members to consider fully the nature and implications of proposals and recommendations before the meeting. A typical committee agenda follows.

NEWBY DISTRICT COUNCIL

Town Hall
Newby
6 February 19—

Dear Sir/Madam

A meeting of the ENVIRONMENTAL SERVICES COMMITTEE will be held on WEDNESDAY, 18 February 19— at 1900 hours in Committee Room B at Newby Town Hall, at which the following business will be transacted.

Yours faithfully

S. T. GREEN

Chief Executive

AGENDA

1. To approve the minutes of the last meeting.
2. Matters arising.
3. Apologies for absence.
4. To consider the monthly report of the Chief Environmental Health Officer (Document A).
5. To consider the report of the Director of Technical Services on proposals to alleviate flooding in Queen Street (Document B).
6. To consider a letter from Newby Catfoods Ltd giving the terms for a sewer easement across the firm's playing fields.

7. To consider a letter from the Kite Residents' Association requesting provision of a public convenience near Jacksonville crossroads.
8. To authorise the demolition of unfit properties at 22 to 30 Barnes Yard.
9. To consider improvement grant applications (Document C).
10. Any other business.

Reports

Reports of various kinds often accompany agenda and these can be of considerable value to members in supplying background information, investigating alternatives and presenting fully-reasoned proposals. Members are able to consider matters covered by reports in detail prior to the committee meeting. Reports may be of various types.

1. *General routine reports of chief officers and departmental heads* providing information on the operation of services and departments. A typical example follows giving an extract from a planning officer's report to a planning committee.

NEWBY DISTRICT COUNCIL
PLANNING COMMITTEE, 18 MAY 19—
PLANNING OFFICER'S REPORT

1. APPLICATIONS FOR DECISION
   The following applications have been received and are submitted for the committee's decision:
   NP/326/78 DOWNHAM AVENUE – Erection of bungalow
   24/4/78 for J. Brown Esq., 36 Chaucer Drive, Newtown.
   [reference
   and date]

   RECOMMENDED that permission be granted subject to the following conditions:
   (1) The access to be constructed, laid out and maintained to the approval of the Director of Technical Services.
   (2) The proposed bungalow shall not be occupied until the applicant has complied with the access requirements.

   The reasons for these conditions are:
   (1) To minimise danger, obstruction and inconvenience to users of the highway and of the premises.

(2) To ensure that a satisfactory means of access is provided at the time the development is carried out, and is satisfactorily maintained thereafter.

The report would then continue with the remainder of the planning applications, followed by other planning matters such as advertisement control, appeals, and building and tree preservation orders.[3]

2. *Detailed reports on items contained in the agenda*, such as the report of the director of technical services on flooding alleviation proposals in item 5 of the typical environmental services committee agenda.
3. *Reports on specific matters* which could, for instance, stem from a decision of the previous committee meeting.

General Requirements of Reports

Officers, when preparing reports for members, should aim at satisfying the following basic criteria.

1. Accuracy – the avoidance of errors or vague statements which can reflect adversely upon the ability of the officer.
2. Simplicity – freedom from technical terms and jargon as far as practicable.
3. Clarity – the contents should be clear and easily read and understood, with ample headings and sub-headings; the avoidance of long paragraphs and sentences.
4. Systematic approach – an orderly presentation and logical sequence; the report often being subdivided into the following parts:
    (i) introduction, possibly incorporating the reasons for the report and the objectives;
    (ii) main body of the report, including a detailed description of existing conditions where appropriate;
    (iii) conclusions and recommendations including, where appropriate, the consideration of alternatives and estimates of cost.
5. Continuity – the report should continue logically from one paragraph to the next and lead into the conclusions and recommendations.
6. Conciseness and completeness – the report must incorporate all relevant matters but be free from superfluous information.
7. Correct grammar and spelling – the report should be grammatically correct and free from spelling mistakes, against a background of falling standards.

Preparations for and Conduct of Meetings

Preliminary Preparations

All documents should be prepared and processed in adequate time for dispatch. An up-to-date record should be maintained of the names and addresses of all committee members and an addressograph machine used for printing envelopes and labels, of which stocks are held for dispatch purposes. Finally, the dispatch of papers should be suitably recorded.

Prior to meetings all appropriate officers will check to ensure that they are fully briefed on all items on the agenda with which they are concerned. The committee clerk will obtain minutes of previous meetings, any appropriate instructions, attendance record sheet, copies of any documents which have been summarised or quoted in the circulated papers, standing orders, ballot papers if voting is possible, and any necessary reference books. The committee clerk normally arranges his papers in the correct sequence and marks them with the relevant agenda item number. Furthermore, a major aim should be to anticipate questions that may be raised at the meeting and to have all the supporting information needed to answer them.

Attendance of Members and Quorum

A correct record of attendances is necessary as an absence of six months can disqualify a member. A register of attendance is normally kept for each committee, commencing each meeting on a separate page headed with the date. The chairman will sign on the uppermost line immediately the meeting commences and the book will then be circulated to each member present for signature. The committee clerk will be responsible for ensuring that late arrivals sign the register. For small committees, the committee clerk may keep the record himself.

The committee clerk must be familiar with the standing orders of his authority, particularly those dealing with chairman, quorum and powers of committees. In the absence of the chairman, the chair is taken by the vice-chairman and in the absence of the latter the committee will appoint its own chairman with the senior member present requesting nominations. If the official chairman subsequently arrives, it is customary for the acting chairman to offer to vacate the chair.

A common quorum for council and committee meetings is one-quarter of the membership for county councils and one-third for district councils. Where a quorum is not achieved at the start of a meeting, but is likely to be obtained later, those present normally proceed with the agenda. When a quorum is obtained, the committee passes a formal resolution approving the business previously transacted on its behalf. When questions cannot be answered adequately, the matter can be adjourned to permit more information to be obtained and placed before the committee at a later meeting.

Conduct of Meetings

Minutes of the previous meetings are normally circulated previously to members and, except in the case of error, will be confirmed as the first item of business, with a copy retained in the official minute book duly signed by the chairman as a true record of the proceedings.

Matters decided by committees should in theory be the subject of motions, whereby the chairman puts each matter to the meeting. Many decisions are carried unanimously, or more often no one opposes the motion and it is carried *nem. con.*, so that voting is unnecessary. Where differences of opinion arise, the chairman will put the matter to the vote and a show of hands follows. Both the chairman and the committee clerk will count the votes for and against and, after comparing totals, the chairman will inform the meeting of its decision. The chairman has a casting vote if the voting is indecisive. An officer who is unable to support a committee's proposals should inform the committee, but after confirmation he is duty bound to implement the proposals unless they are illegal.

Motions

Motions are formal propositions proposed and seconded by members for discussion and adoption. Where a motion is not related directly to an agenda item, standing orders usually require the member to give 'notice of motion' to a prescribed officer a specified number of days before the meeting so that it can be added to the agenda. A motion, on being put to a meeting and carried by a majority of those present and voting, becomes a resolution or decision of the committee or council.

In discussion on a motion, an amendment may be moved and seconded, provided it does not constitute a direct negative. The amendment is then discussed and the proposer of the original motion is given the opportunity to reply. First the amendment is put to the meeting and if it is carried the original motion, as amended by the amendment, becomes a substantive motion for discussion and adoption by the meeting. If it is not carried, the original motion stands and is put to the meeting.

Decisions of committees can be of two forms.

1. Resolutions on matters where the committee has delegated powers.
2. Recommendations where the decision requires confirmation by council or another committee.

Notes of Meetings

Committee clerks keep full notes of proceedings, often in A4-size committee notebooks, and normally head each set of notes with the name of the committee and date, time and place of the meeting. Each item of business is identified separately in the notebook by its agenda number. Adequate and accurate notes should be made of the main points of discussion, including particulars of any motions and amendments, with the names of proposers and seconders and numbers of votes cast. During a lengthy and sometimes confusing debate it may be necessary for the committee clerk to read out the motions and amendments. Often no formal motions are put and the committee clerk drafts a resolution to accord with the views expressed. Any other significant events will also be recorded, such as the chairman vacating the chair for a specific item or a member declaring a pecuniary interest.

The notes should show how every item is resolved, be it by resolution, amendment, recommendation, noting a report, deferring consideration to the next meeting, or whatever. As each minute is subsequently drafted, a line is usually struck through the note of each item and, when drafting is complete, a check is made of the notes and agenda to ensure that each item has been covered.

Minutes

Purposes

The principal purposes of council and committee minutes are as follows.

1. To form the basis of decisions taken at meetings and to provide a permanent and accurate record of the business transacted.
2. On occasions to form the legal basis for determining the local authority's position.
3. To provide a source for day-to-day reference by officers implementing instructions arising from a meeting and, on occasions, embodying amendments to previous directions.
4. In some instances, submitting the approved committee minutes to the parent body will draw its attention to the proceedings

and decisions of the committee with its delegated powers, and thus provide a line of communication between a committee and full council.

Preparation

Minutes shall include details of the date, time and place of the meeting, and names of persons attending and of the chairman of the meeting. The order of items usually follows the agenda. The minutes should be concise but, at the same time, be complete and in sufficient detail to provide adequate information on business transacted by the committee and authority for necessary action to be taken, and to identify the officers who are to take the action.

It is neither practicable nor desirable for the minutes to detail all discussions fully, but the Local Government Act 1972 does require minutes to be kept of proceedings as distinct from decisions. A record of decisions only would constitute a very poor record for future use. Information should be recorded showing how items are introduced and the action decided. For example, a typical minute could read:

The Committee considered a report of the Director of Housing on the condition of gardens on the Fairway Estate.
Resolved:
That the Director of Housing be instructed to approach the tenants of the following dwellings, requesting prompt remedial action, and to submit a further report to the next meeting of the Committee.

The names of proposers and seconders and terms of defeated amendments are not usually recorded in the minutes of committees but are likely to be included in council minutes. Where decisions involve legal matters, such as the making of a compulsory purchase order, the legal implications should be considered and the relevant statutory powers stated. Identifying notes should be inserted in the minutes covering government circulars and other official documents and correspondence which have been submitted to committees and council.

Each minute and each page of minutes should be consecutively numbered for ease of reference. Any committee minutes amended at a later committee meeting must be suitably corrected and such amended minutes signed by the chairman. On the other hand the amendment of a committee recommendation by council would be covered by a marginal note. Reference to circulated reports is done most effectively by including the relevant section or paragraph numbers.

When a full disclosure of information in the minutes could detrimentally affect the local authority's interests, any identifying particulars should be omitted. Attention should also be paid to the implications of the law of libel where enforcement action by the local authority is to be followed by court action.

Draft minutes are usually submitted by the committee clerk to any senior officers involved at the meeting, to secure their general agreement. In this way any errors of fact can usually be eliminated. Reports circulated with the agenda often form an important part of the minutes and are bound with them.

The accuracy of the minutes is of great importance and they should therefore be in a form which effectively prevents the wrongful removal or substitution of pages. Originally, bound books were used, which involved writing out the minutes by hand, using special typewriters which can type in bound books, or pasting sheets of typed or printed minutes on to pages of the book. Loose-leaf books do not suffer from these disadvantages and are permitted by the Local Government Act 1972. For security, a loose-leaf minute book should have a lockable binder, the minutes should be serially numbered through the book and the chairman should sign at the end of the minutes and initial each intervening page.

Under the Local Government Act 1972, a local government elector has the right to inspect the minutes of proceedings of a council and to make a copy or extract. He has no similar right to inspect committee minutes, even those involving delegated powers, except where they have been submitted to the council or where they are expressly made available for inspection by statute, such as under the Education Act 1944 and the National Health Service Act 1946.

Action on Minutes

Where a committee does not have delegated powers it makes recommendations to the council, which may approve, amend, reject or refer it back to the committee for further consideration. Committee decisions and recommendations can be submitted to the council in several ways.

One approach is to submit the minutes, which saves time and gives the council a complete picture of the committee's work. Unfortunately, the minutes may not have been ratified by the committee, are in greater detail than is really necessary and may not provide a very coherent account for the council.

Alternatively a separate report of proceedings can be submitted and, where there is extensive delegation, such reports may be submitted at less frequent intervals, probably quarterly. Advantages are that trivial items can be omitted, while a full account can be given of important matters requiring council decision. The practice with some authorities is to circulate copies of the minutes of all committees to council members and to restrict reports to important matters which are detailed fully with the committee's recommendations. In this way every council member is fully cognisant of the business of all committees, although it does result in the circulation of large quantities of paper. Other authorities make committee minutes available for inspection by council members. A second alternative is to record in the committee minutes only those items which the committee believes should be reported to council.

The committee clerk is responsible for ensuring that any decisions or instructions given by his committee are implemented. A common practice is for the clerk to prepare a statement of action to be taken after each committee meeting, either as a separate document or inserted beside the minutes of the meeting. These can also be used for monitoring progress.

Local Government Staffing

The Local Government Service

Local authorities in England and Wales together spend annually over £5000 million on the provision of services and employ over two million people, approximately half of whom are in the education services as teachers or support staff.[4] The range of activities and specialisms of employees is enormous. The hundreds of local authorities are all independent employers and the staff needs vary with the type, size and functions of the authority. For example, the needs of a metropolitan district with its concentrated population and wide-ranging duties will differ from those of a predominantly rural district council, whose primary function is housing.

As described in Chapter 4 the local government service includes both officers and servants. Officers perform clerical, administrative or professional duties, while servants undertake manual work, although the division becomes rather blurred on occasions. The servants form an important part of the service, both in the large numbers employed and in the nature and quality of their products. Indeed, much of the success of the service depends upon the calibre of the persons employed.

Conditions of Employment

Local authorities are required under the Local Government Act 1972 to appoint such officers as they think necessary for the proper discharge of their functions, and the officers so appointed are to hold office on such reasonable terms and conditions, including remuneration, as the authority thinks fit. As described in Chapter 4, local authorities have special responsibilities with regard to the appointment of statutory officers. An officer can be seconded to another authority after consultation with him.

All officers must account for all money and property when required to do so by the authority, and this liability continues for three months after relinquishing the appointment. Members of councils, except chairmen and vice-chairmen, cannot hold paid office until twelve months after they have ceased to be members. The majority of officers are employed on standard conditions, although a few may be engaged on limited contractual arrangements. Officers are required to give written notice of any pecuniary or other interest, whether direct or indirect, in any existing or proposed contract by the authority. Furthermore, an officer must not through his office or employment accept any fee or reward other than his remuneration.

Personnel Management

The Bains Study Group[5] believed that the local government service tended to lag behind industry and other areas of the public service in its recognition and development of the personnel management function. The Study Group considered that the commonly held view that the establishment or personnel officer controlled the day-to-day administration of salaries and conditions of service and acted as the council's watchdog in respect of staffing claims was far too narrow. The wider approach operating in large industrial enterprises was welcomed, where personnel management aims at promoting the effectiveness of human resources and the creation and maintenance of a climate in which change to the advantage of the employer can be achieved. Activities such as manpower planning, recruitment techniques, post-entry training, career development, salary administration and industrial relations are all important personnel management functions.

To undertake these functions effectively requires a personnel officer as adviser to the chief executive on staffing matters. His proposals would also be subject to close examination by the management team. Personnel management is not an end in itself; its objective is to influence and create an environment in which the authority can recruit and develop the employees it needs to achieve its objectives.[5]

Superannuation

The Local Government Superannuation Acts 1937 and 1953 and

the regulations made under them require all except the smallest local authorities to maintain a superannuation fund, into which both officers and the authority contribute and from which superannuation allowances are paid on retirement to permanent officers and temporary officers with over two years' service and certain servants. Officers and servants carry their accrued superannuation rights with them on securing employment with another authority.

A compulsory retiring age of 65 operates, but employing local authorities can extend an employee's service by a maximum period of one year at a time. There are other superannuation codes covering particular classes of employee, such as teachers. The Superannuation (Miscellaneous Provisions) Act 1948 provides for the preservation of superannuation rights on changes of employment between local government, teaching, civil service and the.colonial service. There is also statutory provision for payment of compensation to those suffering loss of office because of legislative changes.

Conditions of Service

Local authorities are restricted in the extent to which they can prescribe and operate their own terms of employment because of the joint negotiating machinery. Hence the basic local government service conditions and salary scales are determined by national negotiating bodies and the individual local authorities, as employers and parties to the national agreements, implement them. Each local authority has some discretion in determining its staff establishment, and can often select the national salary scale which it considers most appropriate, while it can also make its own appointments and fix its office hours within the nationally prescribed working week.

A National Joint Council for Local Authorities' Administrative, Professional, Technical and Clerical Services was established in 1944 and this represented a major step towards the creation of a municipal civil service, and it secured for the first time a uniform approach to salaries and conditions of service. The National Joint Council consists of employers' representatives from each type of local authority and staff representatives from each of the relevant trade unions, of which the National and Local Government Officers' Association (NALGO) is the largest. There are also provincial councils at district level and local joint committees at branch level, each of which sends one representative of the employers and one of staff to the National Joint Council.

The first national set of conditions of service for local government was produced by the National Joint Council in 1946. It is sometimes referred to as 'the charter' but more usually as the 'purple book', as the conditions are contained in a book with purple covers.[6] These conditions embrace the majority of officers, but exclude most chief officers, who have their own negotiating committees.

These conditions cover a wide range of matters – appointment and promotion, post-entry training, salary and grading provisions, hours and leave, sickness payments and maternity leave, travelling and subsistence, and official conduct and appeals. Appeals against salary gradings, wrongful dismissal or other grievances are decided by the employing authority in the first instance. Where the officer is dissatisfied with the decision, the matter is usually referred to the provincial council as a 'difference'.

Recruitment and Training

Recruitment

For many years local authorities recruited mainly from local secondary schools. These entrants were appointed to junior or trainee posts and worked their way up the establishment of a particular department, often qualifying by part-time study. A very commendable extension of this approach was adopted by Nottinghamshire County Council, whereby an annual intake of trainees spent several weeks in each of the main departments before deciding which department they wished to join. It also gave them the opportunity to see the broad range of activities of the council.

Some specialist officers entered with a university, commercial or professional background. In the 1960s and 1970s many more entrants were graduates from universities and polytechnics, joining the service at a later age, as a result of the large expansion of higher educational facilities.

The National Joint Council conditions of service aimed at establishing the local government service as offering a career likely to attract entrants of the type required for the future needs of local government. It aimed to recruit from the widest possible field, both junior entrants aged 16 or 18 and officers holding university and polytechnic degrees. It is believed that successful recruitment depends on satisfying four important criteria.

1. Sound recruitment practice which eliminates patronage and gives the benefit of competitive selection.
2. Salaries and conditions of service which must not compare unfavourably with those obtainable elsewhere.
3. Adequate post-entry training facilities, both academic and practical.
4. Reasonable facilities for promotion.

The Mallaby Report[7] considered that there was a growing need to recruit graduates as trainees for professional and administrative posts and that local authorities should place increasing emphasis on recruitment from universities and polytechnics. Local authorities should, at the same time, continue to recruit school-leavers who do not proceed to higher education and, as an incentive to recruitment, offer good training schemes and opportunities to obtain administrative and professional qualifications. The Committee recognised the need for local authorities to offer adequate rewards and attractions comparable with those offered by competing employers in order to attract and retain staff of suitable quality.

The Committee believed that local authorities needed to pursue a more positive approach to recruitment by increased liaison with schools careers masters and youth employment officers, arranging holiday attachments for senior school pupils, and paying careful attention to the timing of the approaches to school-leavers and the quality of the publicity material. Local authorities were advised to establish direct contacts with universities, polytechnics and other colleges and their undergraduates and to consider making joint approaches with other local authorities.

Induction

When a new entrant arrives at an office the usual procedure is for him to be received by the section head, shown around the department and be given an account of the work undertaken. It is now generally believed that the newcomer should be given an introductory course on the local government service. In this way he can see the relevance of his own department's work set against the wider background. The courses can also include talks by senior officers, films and visits to local authority services. The form of induction training should be varied to suit the age, ability and background of the new entrant and the work he is to do.[7]

One method of initial training is for the supervisor personally to introduce the new entrant to the work, stage by stage, and only to move on to the next stage when he is certain that the previous stage is clearly understood. Subsequently the newcomer undertakes the work under a reducing amount of supervision. The method whereby a new entrant is attached to a member of staff and instructed to watch him is far less satisfactory, as the newcomer may also copy the member of staff's errors and undesirable attitudes.

Training

The local government service employs more specialists than general administrators. Most officers are given facilities to obtain appropriate qualifications by attendance on day-release and sandwich courses, principally at polytechnics and other colleges, or by taking correspondence courses. For example, junior officers in the technical services department would aim for membership of the Institution of Civil Engineers or the Institution of Municipal Engineers if engaged on highways and transportation, the Royal Town Planning Institute if undertaking town planning, the Royal Institute of British Architects if doing architectural work, and the Royal Institution of Chartered Surveyors if engaged on quantity surveying or on estate management and valuation.

The Bains Study Group[5] considered that the development of training policies required the identification of training needs, knowledge of training theory and practice, and skill in the training process. The Mallaby Committee[7] believed that local authorities should accept responsibility for arranging training facilities and enabling officers to use them. The Committee also recognised the need for continued general education as well as professional training for trainees recruited direct from school. They advised local authorities to make allowance for training needs when fixing departmental staffing levels, to sponsor students on sandwich courses, to second selected officers to other authorities, industry and commerce, and to provide refresher training to keep serving officers abreast of developments in their disciplines and to retrain staff displaced by technological change. Many of these recommendations were being implemented in the early 1970s, but were cut back drastically in the mid-1970s as part of government cuts.

Local Government Training Board

The Board was established in 1966 with representatives from employer and staff organisations, and it has assisted in securing an extension of the training provided for all grades of staff in local government and greater recognition by employing authorities of the great importance of training.

The Board identified the following general objectives.

1. To increase the efficiency of local government by ensuring that sufficient training of suitable quality is given to local authority employees at all levels.

2. To ensure that the cost of training is evenly and fairly spread amongst all local authorities by levies so that all contribute on a fair and intelligible basis to an activity from which all benefit.

The work of the Board includes the following activities.

1. Production of training recommendations.
2. Preparation of training material.
3. Provision of training advice to individual local authorities.
4. Running of experimental courses in conjunction with training officers of provincial councils.
5. Sponsoring of specialist courses at institutions of higher education, such as courses in management for senior staff.
6. Research into and development of new areas connected with training, such as management by objectives and manpower forecasting.

The Board raised its first levy in 1968 and made a systematic examination of training requirements. It allocated a high priority to managerial and supervisory training and to the training of clerical and administrative staff. The Board encourages the provision of more and better 'on the job' training facilities by local authorities.

Staff Development

Selection

The Bains Study Group[5] recognised the importance of making satisfactory selection decisions when appointing new staff. The Group believed that more attention should be paid to man and job specifications, the design of application forms to secure the maximum information relevant to the post and the development and extension of interviewing skills. In the past many staff interviews have been conducted by large committees of council members, unskilled in selection techniques and often having little knowledge of the qualities they are seeking, with the result that the judgements formed are likely to be purely subjective.[4]

The Mallaby Committee[7] recommended seeking advice from outside assessors, in addition to the chief executive, when appointing principal officers and their deputies, and keeping these interviewing panels small. The Committee believed that principal officers should have responsibility for selecting and appointing staff up to and including third-tier level.

Promotion and Career Prospects

The Bains Study Group[5] advocated that local authorities should adopt a more positive approach in developing the potential of members of their staff, and favoured secondment arrangements.

The Mallaby Committee[7] believed that the prospects of the school-leaver trainee, when he has qualified, should be the same as those of his graduate counterpart, that the technician should be given a proper place beside the professional officer, and that there should be good career prospects for lay administrative officers up to second- and third-tier positions where practicable, with status and salaries equivalent to professional staff at these levels. The Committee recommended that chief executive posts should be open to all professions, including lay administrative officers, although this latter recommendation has not been very favourably received by most chief officers. Knowles[4] has described how chief officers need increasingly to possess managerial know-how rather than professional qualifications.

Cunningham and Fahey[8] have described how local government is unique as a major employer in that most senior posts have been traditionally reserved for professionally qualified staff, unlike the Civil Service, where the professional specialist provides advice to the administrator, who acts in a general managerial capacity. On a series of courses for middle-ranking local authority administrative staff, the most quoted work-problem was the relationship with professional staff, while professional staff rarely gave this as a problem area.

Ideally local authorities should have a planned career-development policy linked to a system of manpower planning. In this way officers will be provided with suitable career opportunities, related to their potential and the needs of the authority. Staff-development schemes usually place responsibility for each officer's development upon his immediate superior. This should be linked with a staff-appraisal system to keep the authority suitably informed about the quality and potentiality of its staff.[4]

Manpower Planning

The personal record of each officer should provide personal particulars and details of the post held, qualifications, training and career history. This information is required as a basis for forecasting future manpower needs in conjunction with the authority's development programme. It is important to know whether manpower is being used effectively and to determine appropriate staffing levels.

Preparing realistic forecasts of future staffing requirements is difficult. Manpower planning will however identify events which may cause problems, such as the simultaneous retirement of a number of key officers or the absence of suitable officers for promotion at specific periods of time. Hence manpower planners require details of age, qualifications and experience distribution for each department, and employment trends for various categories of staff. The main objectives are to determine recruitment intakes, assess future accommodation requirements, plan career development, secure efficient use of manpower, avoid redundancies and assess optimum training levels.[4]

References

1. DEPARTMENT OF THE ENVIRONMENT (Ministry of Housing and Local Government) *Model Standing Orders: Proceedings and Business of Local Authorities* (H.M.S.O., 1968).
2. JACKSON, W. E., *The Structure of Local Government in England and Wales* (Longman, 1966).
3. SEELEY, I. H., *Municipal Engineering Practice* (Macmillan, 1967).
4. KNOWLES, R. S. B., *Modern Management in Local Government* (Butterworth, 1971).
5. STUDY GROUP ON LOCAL AUTHORITY MANAGEMENT STRUCTURES, *The New Local Authorities: Management and Structure* – the Bains Report (H.M.S.O., 1972).
6. NATIONAL JOINT COUNCIL FOR LOCAL AUTHORITIES' ADMINISTRATIVE, PROFESSIONAL, TECHNICAL AND CLERICAL SERVICES, *The Scheme of Conditions of Service* (8th edn 1976; subject to partial revision from time to time).
7. *Report of the Committee on the Staffing of Local Government* – the Mallaby Report (H.M.S.O., 1967).
8. CUNNINGHAM, I. and FAHEY, U., 'Administrators and Professionals in Local Government', *Local Government Studies*, October 1976.

CHAPTER SEVEN

LOCAL GOVERNMENT FINANCE

Financial Needs of Local Authorities

All local authorities need funds to finance the wide range of public services which they provide. The powers of local authorities to spend money in this way are prescribed by statute and, in general, they are permitted to spend money only on activities which are within their statutory powers, except for a small rate to be spent for the benefit of their areas and inhabitants generally.[1] Local government expenditure in the financial year 1975–6 amounted to approximately £10 million, and this accounted for about 30 per cent of all public expenditure. The collection, spending and control of such a large sum of money requires the establishment of efficient administrative arrangements.

The early 1970s saw a large increase in local authority expenditure, which stemmed mainly from the following factors.

1. Central government demands for the improvement and extension of local public services.
2. An increasing public demand for a higher standard of service.
3. An increase in population.
4. A proportionately greater increase in the young and old, both sectors making greater demands on social services.
5. The effect of inflation.[2]

By the mid-1970s the situation had changed dramatically. Against a background of high inflation, increasing unemployment and large cuts in public expenditure, local authorities were subjected to substantial reductions in capital expenditure and a reduced rate of growth in revenue expenditure.

Budgets

Each local authority in the latter part of the financial year (January and February) formulates a detailed set of estimates of income and expenditure for each service for the following financial year commencing on 1 April. These estimates after approval by the spending committees are submitted in their entirety to the finance committee for detailed scrutiny. The finance committee subsequently submits the amended estimates to the full council and these will form the basis for the next year's rate assessment.

Expenditure is subdivided under two main heads – capital and revenue. Capital expenditure entails the purchase of an asset such as houses, a school, new offices, a highway or a refuse vehicle, which will give service over a considerable period of time. Local authorities usually borrow money to finance capital projects, and the loan period varies with the type of asset, typical periods being 60 years for buildings, 30 years for sewers, 20 years for highways and seven years for vehicles. Small items of capital expenditure can be charged to the revenue account. Revenue expenditure includes staff salaries, operatives' wages, and the day-to-day expense of operating essential services, and these costs are met out of rates and other sources of income. The cost of loan repayments or debt charges will also be included in revenue expenditure.

Each local authority is responsible for meeting its own expenditure but subject to central government assistance. The rate requirement will be determined by deducting central government assistance in the form of grants and subsidies from the total annual expenditure. Some expenditure on specialised services, which it would be uneconomic and inefficient for every authority to provide, is pooled. The services are provided by a limited number of authorities but payment is made by all authorities. Typical examples are the provision of advanced further education and teacher-training. The main objection is that an authority providing a pooled service may have little incentive to economise if it is meeting only a small part of the cost, while at least one providing authority has argued that it has a general responsibility to keep expenditure on the pooled service down to an absolute minimum and so reduce the financial burden on other authorities in times of economic stringency.

The expenditure of local authorities increased significantly on reorganisation in 1974 – in many areas in the order of 50 per cent and in some areas almost 100 per cent – resulting in considerable public outcry. These increases resulted from a number of factors, including recruitment of more officers, improvements in salaries, pensions to officers retiring early, increased allowances to councillors and acquisition of new premises and equipment. In addition the charges levied by the new water authorities for the water-supply and sewage-treatment functions exceeded considerably the costs of the local authorities for the provision of these services previously.[3]

Main Sources of Local Government Income

Local authorities would achieve greater status and independence if they could meet the whole of their expenditure from local sources. Unfortunately this is not practicable and they rely heavily upon assistance from central government. Increased central government contributions to local government finance has been accompanied by greater control of local authority activities.

Central government needs to supplement local government revenues because most local authority services are quasi-national in character. For example, education and police have important national implications. Local revenues need to be further supplemented because the comparative rigidity of the rate base cannot keep pace with local government spending. Most central government taxes have their base adjusted automatically in times of inflation so that unchanged percentage rates of tax produce increased tax income. The tax base for rates increases only when there is a general revaluation of property or a significant number of new buildings erected.[4]

Grants-in-aid can also be given to support new services and their development, to compensate local authorities for relief granted to ratepayers, and to assist in equalising the financial resources of local authorities so that a common standard of service can be provided.

Rateable values are not evenly distributed, hence without assistance from central government the less well endowed authorities would need to levy higher rate poundages than the wealthier authorities to provide the same standard of service. A search for alternative sources of local revenue has not been very successful. There have been a number of changes in the method of central government grant distribution but Little[4] has shown that insufficient investigations have been made into determining the optimum level of central government contribution. There is a need to secure the right balance – too little central government grant and too much local tax will produce opposition from the ratepayers and the reverse could result in some loss of local independence and greater pressure on local taxation. To overcome the deficiencies of local finance, central government grants have been progressively increased, rising from 54 per cent of net local authority expenditure in England and Wales in 1967 to 65 per cent in 1976.

The inability of local authorities to obtain sufficient finance from local sources to meet the expenditure of expanding services could provide a reason for transferring further services from local authorities to other agencies. Furthermore, if local authorities receive an excessive proportion of their finance from central funds, they may be demoted to becoming merely agents of central government, with little discretion over how the money is spent. The aim of central government might justifiably be to provide local services to a uniform standard throughout the country if financed from national funds, and specific local needs would then be ignored.

The function of local government must surely be to provide local services to meet local needs and to fail to achieve this negates the very *raison d'être* of local government, as uniform services might better be provided by central government agencies. Yet it is widely known that the needs of different districts vary greatly and that local people are best fitted to identify and meet these local needs. There are also such desirable features as local initiative and pride, which we destroy at our peril.

Sources of local revenue are shown in Table 3. The largest source of local finance is the product of rates, which constitute a local

TABLE 3 *Sources of local revenue*

Year	Rateable value	Total revenue income	Sources of total revenue income		
			Rates	Government grants	Miscellaneous
	£m	£m	£m	£m	£m
1923–4	236	341	143	75	123
1933–4	274	446	148	122	176
1943–4	317	739	204	228	307
1953–4	347	1 176	392	414	370
1963–4	2 040	2 772	923	1 022	827
1970–1	2 440	6 258	1 640	2 284	2 334
1971–2	2 493	7 293	1 912	2 654	2 727
1972–3	2 545	8 215	2 180	3 135	2 900
1973–4	6 583	9 830	2 415	3 897	3 518

SOURCE: Department of the Environment, *Local Government Financial Statistics (England and Wales) 1973–74.*

tax levied on occupiers of property in the area. This source is supported by other forms of local finance such as proceeds from trading services, like local transport, and income from various other facilities of which car parks, swimming baths, theatres, evening classes, library fines and council house rents are typical examples.

Central government financial assistance takes various forms of which the largest and most important is the rate support grant, which is a general grant aimed at helping all local services. Its amount is calculated using a complicated formula which includes the size of the authority, the number of children and old people, rateable value and similar factors. Other grants, such as housing subsidies, are confined to a particular service. These forms of government assistance are examined in more detail later in this chapter.

In addition local authorities need to borrow large sums of money to finance capital projects and these loans are obtained from a variety of sources, as listed below. The local government outstanding loan debt in 1975 was £25 billion.[5]

1. Public Works Loan Board, an independent statutory body, essentially a lender of last resort – percentage of loan debt, 38 per cent.
2. Short-term market – initial borrowing of less than one year – mainly from banks, building societies, insurance companies, industry and commerce, offering to investors an efficient service coupled with absolute security and attractive rates of interest – percentage of loan debt, 13 per cent.
3. Local authority negotiable bonds or 'yearlings', through the discount market and private investors – percentage of loan debt, 3 per cent.
4. Stock issues often offered to the public at very attractive rates by the larger local authorities with Treasury consent and minimum issues of £3 million – percentage of loan debt, 7 per cent.
5. Internal advances and other miscellaneous loans – percentage of loan debt, 11 per cent.
6. Bonds and mortgages – about 20 per cent is obtained from local subscribers as a result of newspaper advertisements, and the remainder from the money market – percentage of loan debt, 28 per cent.[6]

Rating

Nature and Method of Operation

Rates are levied on the occupiers of real property. Occupation to be rateable must embrace legal possession, permanence and beneficial occupation.[7] The amount which falls due in respect of any property or 'hereditament' depends primarily on its rateable value.

The original basis of assessment, which still underlies the law, is the rent which a tenant, holding the hereditament on a tenancy from year to year, might reasonably be expected to pay, on the conditions which were common on the letting of house property, namely that the landlord paid the cost of repairs and insurance and the tenant paid tenant's rates and taxes. This is called the 'gross value' of the hereditament.[8]

Rateable values are however based on the occupier's liability, and hence the cost of repairs and insurance have to be deducted from 'gross value' to produce 'net annual value' or 'rateable value'. There is a standard scale of allowances derived from the Valuation (Statutory Deductions) Order 1973. The rateable values are assessed by the Inland Revenue on the basis of rental value, which has become increasingly difficult to apply because of the absence of free rents and the extension of owner–occupation. Alternative techniques have also to be applied with some other classes of property, and the Local Government Act 1974 made provision for the Minister to specify the method of determining the rateable values of certain public utilities.

District councils are the rating authorities and they prescribe the rate in the pound (£) to be levied on the occupiers of property and are responsible for the collection of rates. County and parish councils are not rating authorities and they issue precepts for the amounts they require on the rating authorities in their area, who add these amounts to the district rates. Although there is only one general rate in any area, rating authorities may levy additional items in any part of their area to cover expenditure benefiting only that particular area.

The rating authority must specify in the rate demand note the purposes for which the rate is levied and the amounts attributable to precepts. In certain instances, owners may be rated instead of occupiers, to avoid collecting large numbers of small amounts from ratepayers, and the owner is then entitled to a discount described as a 'compounding allowance'. Rating authorities can also allow discounts, to all ratepayers or to domestic ratepayers only, where rates are paid by a specified date, although the desirability of this practice has been questioned. To enforce payment of rates, the rating authority can apply to the Justices for a distress warrant and ultimately for commitment to prison.

An example will serve to illustrate the way in which rates are operated.

		£m
total estimated expenditure of the district council		12
add county precept		3
	total	15
less expected income from grants, subsidies, trading income and all other sources		9
total to be found from rates		6

Assuming the rateable value of the district to be £12 million, then the rate in the £ to be paid by each ratepayer will be 50p.

If a ratepayer occupies a dwelling with a rateable value of £250, his annual rate demand will be 250×50p = £125.

Rate demands are issued twice annually but domestic ratepayers have the right to pay their rates in at least ten instalments. The domestic element of the rate support grant requires rating authorities to reduce the rate in the £ on dwelling houses and certain other properties (mixed properties) by an amount fixed annually in the rate grant order, and by the mid-1970s these had accrued to substantial amounts.

In 1929, agricultural land was derated entirely and industrial and freight transport hereditaments were relieved of three-quarters of their rate liability, which was subsequently reduced to one-half in 1958. In 1963 the derating of these latter hereditaments ceased as industry was far more prosperous than before the war. Some object to the principle of derating and argue that any relief to particular categories of ratepayers is better given as subsidies. Agricultural land and outbuildings still have complete exemption, although farmhouses are subject to normal domestic rates.

Under the Local Government Act 1966 rating authorities could by resolution decide to rate unoccupied properties, but the resolution had to remain in force for a period of seven years. The owner of an unoccupied property then became liable for half of the rates payable on the property after the premises had been continuously unoccupied for three months, or six months in the case of new property. The Local Government Act 1974 introduced a more flexible approach, whereby the seven-year time limit was rescinded and the rating authority was given discretion in the selection of pro portion of rate payable and the areas and classes of property to which it was applied.

The 1974 Act also introduced a penalty surcharge on commercial property if 80 per cent of it had not been used for its appropriate purpose for six months and the owner had not 'tried his best' to let it. The principal aim was to prevent office blocks being kept vacant for long periods. The surcharge commences at 100 per cent of the full rates for the first twelve months of non-use, rising progressively by 100 per cent per annum thereafter. The surcharge is levied as rates in addition to any rate or any empty property rate due. The rating authority in deciding whether the owner has 'tried his best' to let the property will have regard to the following factors

1. Rent required in comparison with similar properties in the area.
2. Terms of the proposed lease.
3. Willingness to let in parts.

4. Standing of the estate agents engaged.
5. Extent of advertising.

The owner can appeal against the surcharge to the Crown Court, and surcharges are registered as local land charges.

Certain properties are wholly or partly exempt from rates by statute. For example, religious buildings are wholly exempt and charities receive 50 per cent rate relief, although rating authorities may reduce or remit the balance. Crown land is exempt but the Treasury makes an equivalent payment, while other exempt properties include public parks, lighthouses and residences of ambassadors and their servants. The discretionary power to reduce or remit rates also applies to certain non-profit-making organisations, such as scientific, literary, social and educational societies. Public bodies are liable for rates on properties they occupy for the discharge of their functions, even though they may incur expenditure without any compensating monetary return.

Valuations and Valuation Lists

Valuation for rating is a complicated process and three categories of value are involved: gross, net annual and rateable. The general principle is that gross value is equivalent to the rent at which the premises could reasonably be expected to be let if the landlord was responsible for repairing and insuring the property and the tenant paid the usual tenant's rates and taxes. Net annual value is based on the assumption that the tenant, rather than the landlord, meets the cost of repairs and insurance. Rateable value is generally the same as net annual value except for certain special classes of property such as tithes and land covered with water.[1]

The operation of rent control ever since the First World War has made the calculation of rateable value difficult because of the absence of free rents, and this has been accentuated by the growth of owner–occupation. Prior to 1948 valuations for rating were undertaken locally and there was appeals machinery which attempted to secure uniformity of approach within counties. There was a lack of uniformity in valuation methods throughout the country and many houses built between the wars were assessed at figures below their appropriate values, resulting in unfortunate variations in rating valuations throughout the country.

The first move towards increased uniformity in rating practice stemmed from the Local Government Act 1948, whereby valuation work was transferred from local authorities to the Board of Inland Revenue. It was also recognised that there was a need to redefine the basis of valuation to secure a more uniform approach. The

1948 Act introduced a new approach to the valuation of dwelling houses, introducing a percentage of capital cost in place of estimated rental value. This approach proved to be impracticable and the basis of valuation of dwelling houses was changed in 1953 to the rent at which they might reasonably have been expected to be let in June 1939. Other classes of property were valued on current rental values. The first valuation lists incorporating these changes were introduced in 1956 and they imposed heavier burdens on the occupiers of shops, offices and similar properties. The Rating and Valuation Act 1957 accordingly derated these properties by 20 per cent for the period up to the next revaluation (1963).

The Rating and Valuation Act 1961 secured a revaluation of all property at current values, which became effective in 1963. The next revaluation, planned for 1968, was deferred to 1973; revaluations are expensive and labour-intensive activities. The General Rate Act 1975 postponed the 1978 revaluation to 1980 and empowered the Minister to secure further yearly postponements by statutory instrument. The purpose of the deferment was to prevent the Layfield Committee's inquiry into local government finance being prejudiced.

Although rating authorities (district councils) remain responsible for the levying and collection of rates, they have no functions in connection with the preparation of valuation lists. Nevertheless, they can make proposals for the inclusion of hereditaments in the valuation list where the valuation officer has declined to do so and they can object to proposed assessments.

Appeals against assessments of the valuation officer are first heard by a local Valuation Court and there is a right of appeal against the Court's decision to the Lands Tribunal, and from there only on a point of law to the Court of Appeal and thence to the House of Lords.

Merits and Demerits of Rating

The principal merits of rating are as follows.

1. Rates have been operating for several centuries and are generally accepted as an integral and necessary part of local government.
2. Rates are assessed on property, which is generally accepted as the ideal base for local taxes, being visible and stable.
3. It is difficult to avoid paying rates.
4. Rates provide a realistic and reasonably stable base from which a local authority can make reasonable forecasts of likely future income, with a substantial, certain and predictable yield.
5. Rates are relatively easy and inexpensive to collect, and are administered at less than 2 per cent of yield.

6. Rates are obtained locally and are unique to local government, and this strengthens the position of local authorities.
7. Each occupier of property pays rates and is thereby encouraged to take an interest in local government.
8. The burden of rates is not excessive for the majority of ratepayers.
9. Rates are a form of tax that is generally reasonably well understood.
10. Rates tend to encourage fuller occupation of property.

The demerits of rating are considerable.

1. Rates tend to operate as a disincentive to the improvement of property, as improvements increase the occupier's rate liability.
2. Rates do not produce resources which are necessarily related to needs and so adjustments are made through the resources element of the rate support grant.
3. The level of revenue is largely unresponsive to changes in price levels and the needs of local authorities and does not keep pace with the falling purchasing power of money.
4. Rates are more evident than other forms of taxation and are usually demanded as comparatively large sums at six-monthly intervals.
5. It is difficult to make valuations for rating purposes with a restricted free market in rented property, and periodic revaluations are necessary.
6. As a tax on the occupation of property rates increase the cost of housing accommodation and could conceivably encourage low housing standards and overcrowding.
7. Rates are relatively regressive and inelastic, and they fall unevenly on different classes of ratepayer.
8. The charges are not related to the extent of use of services.

Rate Rebates and Other Forms of Assistance

Rating authorities have power to grant a discount to ratepayers who pay the whole of the rate before a specified date, although this concession may be restricted to domestic ratepayers. The objective is to encourage early payment of rates to produce funds to meet the payment of salaries, purchase of materials and other expenditure early in the financial year and so avoid borrowing and the payment of interest charges. Some argue that this provision operates unfairly against poorer ratepayers who are unable to take advantage of the concession. In practice only few rating authorities allow discounts.

Under the Rating Act 1966, domestic ratepayers have the right to pay rates in at least ten monthly instalments with the final instalment in February. The ratepayer has the choice as to method of payment, but if he wishes to exercise this option he must give written notice to the rating authority within a prescribed period.

The Rating Act 1966 also introduced a system of rate rebates for domestic ratepayers with low incomes. In the first year of introduction the sums claimed amounted to one-half of those anticipated. The Local Government Act 1974 introduced a new statutory rate rebate scheme, which tends to follow the arrangements for rent rebates and rent allowances introduced under the Housing Finance Act 1972. The new proposals extend rate relief further up the income scale and the new arrangements ease the administrative work of local authorities. The rating authority is entitled to receive a grant of 90 per cent of the cost of rate rebates.

Reforms

Hepworth[1] has identified five reforms of the rating system in the 1960s and 1970s, all of which have been described earlier in this chapter – namely: rate rebates; instalment payments; ability to grant discount to domestic ratepayers; discretionary power to rate empty property; and introduction of 'two-level' rates, one for domestic ratepayers and the second for all other ratepayers.

The Royal Institute of Public Administration[9] recommended in 1956 that all derating should cease and that rates should be supplemented by three new sources of local revenue.

1. A limited type of local income tax recoverable through employers and with business and professional profits taxed on the basis of returns to Inland Revenue.
2. The levying of entertainments tax to be transferred from the Exchequer to local authorities; this tax was abandoned in 1956.
3. Levying of motor vehicle licences to be transferred to local authorities.

The Institute also raised the rather vexed question of the possible extension of municipal trading services to cinemas, theatres, restaurants, public houses, laundries and other facilities. These proposals raise fundamental issues as to the desirability of extending local authority services in these directions. Doubtless these suggestions for additional sources of revenue and other proposals described later in the chapter stem from the increasing dependence of local authorities on central government finance.

Financial Relations with Central Government

Local authorities receive financial assistance from central

government in three main ways: grants, subsidies and loans. These sources of income accounted for just over two-thirds of local government expenditure in England and Wales in the mid-1970s. In its turn local authority expenditure accounted for about one-third of all public expenditure.

In this situation it is only natural that the Government is anxious to ensure that local authorities obtain value for money and feels a need to undertake a satisfactory minimum level of supervision of the administration and financing of local authority services. At the same time the control must not be so detailed or extensive that it seriously restricts local authorities' freedom of action. Some conflicts of interests nationally and locally are bound to occur from time to time and the aim should be to minimise these as far as practicable.

The extent of central financial assistance to local authorities is also influenced by prescribed or accepted levels of service and whether particular services are primarily local or national in character. There is a growing belief that local authorities are too much dependent on central government funding and that they may lose much of their independence and freedom of action if this trend continues. Each of the three main forms of central government financial assistance will now be considered in more detail.

Grants

The most popular form of grant is the block grant, which was first introduced in 1929. Block or general grants are not earmarked for any specific service, whereas specific grants are to be spent on particular services and are usually calculated on a percentage basis. The Local Government Act 1948 replaced the block grants by specific percentage grants, but in the following decade the percentage grants were the subject of considerable criticism both from the Treasury, which disliked the open-ended spending commitment, and the local authority associations, which saw loss of freedom.[10]

The Local Government Act 1958 abolished percentage grants and substituted two new grants towards local authority services, namely a general grant, which was not directly related to the expenditure of local authorities, and a rate deficiency grant. This general approach was further extended and simplified in the Local Government Act 1966, which aimed at reducing the rate burden, which had been rising at a faster rate than national income, and at securing a fairer distribution of Exchequer assistance among local authorities. The general and rate deficiency grants were replaced by a rate support grant, although a few new specific grants were also introduced covering such activities as development or redevelopment of areas, acquisition of land for public open space, and utilising derelict land.

The rate support grant introduced in 1967 became the main source of financial assistance to local authorities. Each year the Minister estimates the total amount of grants, excluding housing subsidies, to be paid to local authorities. The total sum to be allocated in specific grants is then deducted from the total grants sum and the balance is distributed as rate support grant. The relationship between the aggregate grant and relevant local authority expenditure was not prescribed and it started at 54 per cent in 1967–8 rising progressively to 66.5 per cent in 1976–7. The Government felt obliged to reduce this to 61 per cent in 1977–8 as part of the cuts in public expenditure, and the problems resulting from this are discussed later in the chapter.

The rate support grant is made up of three basic elements – needs, resources and domestic. The needs element replaced the former general grant and is calculated on a formula which takes into account the population and population density of the area, proportions of children under five, school children and elderly people, and road mileage. The resources element is paid to local authorities with resources lower than the national average and replaced the former rate deficiency grant. The domestic element reimburses the cost of reducing rate poundages for domestic ratepayers.

The Local Government Act 1974 provided for greater flexibility in the distribution of the rate support grant, with annual reviews to take account of rising price levels and other related matters. It also introduced some new supplementary grants and rating changes, such as revised rebate and empty property rating arrangements, and a new scale of deductions from gross to rateable value; and the effect of minor improvements on rateable values between revaluations is to be disregarded.

Hart and Garner[8] have identified four main reasons for grant aid to local authorities.

1. To stimulate a new service.
2. To relieve the increased burden of rates resulting from new services.
3. To compensate local authorities for loss of income arising from attempts to cure defects in the law of rating by giving relief to certain classes of ratepayers.
4. To attempt to equalise the financial resources of local authorities to ensure their capacity for maintaining a common standard of service throughout the country.

Subsidies

Another form of central government funding of local authority services is that of Exchequer subsidies. The most significant are those relating to housing, which in 1975–6 accounted for 49.8 per cent of London local authority housing revenue accounts and 40.2 per cent for other local authorities in England and Wales. Rate fund contributions amounted to 17.5 and 10.1 per cent respectively and the balance of the expenditure was met by rebated rents and other income.[11]

The Housing and Works Committee of the London Boroughs Association believed these arrangements to be inadequate both in terms of capital expenditure and in subsidies, with the result that in London the areas of highest stress have inadequate resources, insufficient government support, and no hope of solving their problems within the existing framework. Problems were exacerbated in the early 1970s as building costs rose faster than the general price level. The Association considered that direct Exchequer grants should meet any deficit arising from a reasonable overall level of rents, with rate fund contributions confined to items in the housing revenue account, such as welfare, which could be properly financed by all ratepayers. A stable and simpler form of subsidy structure is advocated, with the Government bearing the full cost of implementing the national scales of rent rebates and allowances.[11]

Loans

The third source of local government finance is loans, which are obtained principally from the open market, the Public Works Loan Commissioners and the authorities' own internal resources, such as reserves and superannuation funds.

Local authorities borrow money for two main purposes – to meet expenditure pending receipt of rates, and to finance large capital projects. Temporary loans for revenue purposes do not require government sanction but capital loans do and they must be redeemed within the statutory periods stated in the loan sanction. The Government determines periodically the proportions of loans that can be borrowed from the Public Works Loan Board.

The tendency is for the smaller and less prosperous local authorities to borrow mainly from the Public Works Loan Board. When interest rates are reasonable local authorities may be attracted to issuing stock covering substantial sums loaned for long periods. Short-term loans are normally obtained through the money market or from banks.[3]

Views diverge on the role to be played by central government in respect of local government borrowing. Some feel that as most loans are required to finance national programmes, the Government should assist borrowing and possibly offer favourable rates of interest. The Government aims at co-ordinating the borrowing arrangements of local authorities but wants them to find their own sources to a significant extent.

Financial Problems of Local Authorities in the mid-1970s

The Government reduced the rate support grant from 66.5 to 61 per cent of relevant local authority expenditure in 1977–8. Coupled with annual inflation of about 15 per cent, this means that local authorities would have to increase rates substantially to maintain services at the previous year's level. Additional grants to meet pay and price increases were limited to 10 per cent, well below the expected rate of inflation. In these conditions a general reduction in local authority services seemed inevitable. Department of Education and Science Circular 14/76 set out the reduced rate support implications for education: an estimated overall reduction of 20 000 to 30 000 employees – it was hoped by natural wastage, although this was little consolation to unemployed graduates and certified teachers from teacher training establishments. Planned capital expenditure programmes were also the subject of substantial cuts. Commercial and industrial rates continued at 18.5p more in the pound than domestic rates in England and 36p in Wales, which had already caused problems with some commercial developments. A survey of London office accommodation costs showed that rates as a percentage of rents for prime office accommodation had risen from 27 to 43 per cent in Victoria and from 24 to 45 per cent in Mayfair between 1970 and 1977.[12]

The financial year 1977–8 saw substantial rate increases in many parts of the country (40 per cent in Liverpool and 30 per cent in Oxfordshire) while other authorities were cutting back reserves and so deferring large rate increases to future years, despite a substantial lowering of services. Many local authorities were reducing road and building maintenance, cutting teaching staffs and generally lowering standards, which in many cases will result in greater expenditure in future years.

The Government recommended local authorities to increase hostel and canteen charges at colleges, to reduce spending on old people's and children's homes and to require tenants of local authority dwellings to undertake redecorations and minor internal home maintenance themselves. Berkshire County Council proposed to meet the reduced grant aid and rising costs by discontinuing resurfacing

of roads, closing some library services and divisional education
offices, reducing public transport grants, and terminating the
appointments of 400 'dinner ladies' and transferring their duties
to the already overburdened teachers.[13]

Alternative Sources of Local Authority Income

The Fabian Society[14] has described how local government finance
and taxation form part of the national system and their day-to-day
operation must not frustrate national economic policy. The Society
saw the need for an additional local tax which fitted into this concept
and yet allowed individual local authorities sufficient financial
freedom to preserve their autonomy and political accountability
to their electors. The Society believed that rates would continue to
be the principal local tax and that grants would remain an indis-
pensable feature of the local government system. The Society was
searching for a tax with a genuine local flavour – one related to
local possessions, as the rate; to local incomes or earnings, such
as local income tax; or to activities within the area, such as sales,
purchases or gambling. Yields should ideally be reasonably stable,
be within the taxpayer's ability to pay and not vary too widely in
relation to different authorities' responsibilities.

A government White Paper[15] issued at the same time (1971)
explored the various ways of matching local government income
with the rising cost of the services which it was expected to provide.
For rates to increase faster than incomes would be resented by local
electors, while continually to increase the proportion of local
expenditure met by grants could result in less responsibility
remaining in the hands of local people. The other alternative is,
in common with the Fabian approach,[14] to find new local taxes.

The White Paper recognised the need for substantial government
control of the capital expenditure of local authorities, which might
otherwise reach excessive levels. Current arrangements probably give
sufficient flexibility and allow as much local freedom as is
reasonably practicable. Capital projects in the 'key sector' – those
where national considerations and the need for maintenance of
minimum standards weigh heavily – are controlled through programmes agreed with the departments responsible. For other projects
each authority or group of authorities is given a block allocation
for each year to spend as it likes in the 'locally determined sector'.

The financial burden on local authorities could be reduced by
transferring responsibility for some services from local to central
government or by having local managerial responsibility coupled
with central financial responsibility. Some argue that this approach

could be applied to education but it would encounter problems in operation, as local authorities are responsible for the staffing and organisation of schools and expenditure decisions involve the allocation of various resources – teachers, buildings and equipment. The separation of managerial and financial aspects is not really practicable.

The White Paper[15] examined various alternatives sources of additional revenue and each is now considered in turn.

Local Income Tax

This tax could either be assessed and collected locally on information supplied by the Inland Revenue, or have the tax rate fixed by the local authority with assessment and collection by the Inland Revenue. Both systems would necessitate personal information being transmitted by the Inland Revenue to local authorities and changes in the present strict rules of confidentiality, and some duplication of existing central machinery. Its main advantage is that demands on individuals are more closely related to ability to pay than is the case with rates. The Fabian Society[14] also described the further advantages of a productive tax which keeps pace with local incomes and secures payments from lodgers who escape rates. Its complications are lessened by the advent of computers.

Local Sales Tax

This would be charged on retail sales from all shops and other retail businesses, except perhaps the smallest. Different tax levels in different areas could cause serious problems and difficulties would arise with mail-order firms and direct sales by manufacturers and discount traders. It would produce a high return related to current economic activity, but its feasibility alongside centrally-operated VAT is questionable. This tax is selective but can also be regressive in taxing living standards involving an inflationary element.

Local Employment or Payroll Tax

This constitutes an alternative to local income tax as a means of sharing with central government some part of taxes related to earnings. The larger firms operating in more than one local authority district would have to keep separate employment records related to taxing locality. Such a tax would have less effect on the cost of living than a sales tax but greater effect on industrial costs.

Motor Fuel Duty

This tax is related directly to the use of motor transport. A simple transfer of the motor fuel duty would result in local authorities taking over the collection completely, with power to impose different rates. As an alternative, central government might continue to collect the bulk of the duty and distribute the receipts among local authorities. Because of the large number of retail outlets it would be expensive to administer and susceptible to evasion. It would curtail the central government's scope for regulating the national economy, and different rates of duty in different areas could distort the returns.

Motor Vehicle Duties

The collection of motor vehicle duties, long undertaken by local authorities, was in 1977 being transferred to a central computer system, and this should in time produce staff savings and aid enforcement. The White Paper[15] saw difficulties in transfer to local government because of the ease with which the operational base of goods vehicles can be moved, the complicated structure of rates and their importance for national transport policy. The Fabian Society[14] by comparison saw motor vehicle duties as a natural subject for local taxation, vehicles being local possessions, and the duties providing a widely spread source of income which is relatively cheap to collect.

Super-rating

The White Paper[15] suggested that the shortfall in domestic rate yield could be met by local authorities levying a higher rate poundage on the rateable value of non-domestic properties than on that of domestic premises, involving no additional administrative costs or problems. This practice is in effect currently being operated through the domestic relief element in the rate support grant.

Surcharges on Rates for Earning Non-householders

There are a large number of people with earnings or other income who make no direct contribution to local revenues as they are not, for rating purposes, occupiers of property. It could be argued with some justification that residents of hotels, boarding houses and the like pay their share of rates through accommodation charges. The administrative costs of operating a surcharge would be substantial for a relatively small yield.

Site Value Rating

Rates are a tax on the occupation of land and buildings and are charged on the rental value of property as it exists. With site value rating, rates would be levied on the market rental of the site on the assumption that it was available for the most profitable permitted development and should increase the yield of rates significantly.

Arguments put forward in favour of the tax are that the economic rent of the site is created by the community and not the owner and hence it is right for the community to recover a share of it. It would also encourage owners to develop their land more quickly and, unlike rates, would not discourage improvements. Arguments against the tax include the fact that it taxes prospective and potential resources regardless of the owner's ability to pay, when indeed the resources might not always be realisable, and that it could be levied only on owners. There are also practical difficulties – amenities would be priced out of existence, valuation problems would provide scope for grievance and litigation, and owners of land are less easily identified than occupiers, making collection and recovery more difficult.

Rating of Agriculture

Agriculture represents one substantial class of property that is still exempt from rates, stemming from when agriculture was a depressed industry, which is no longer the case. Its valuation would however pose a substantial valuation task needing the services of scarce professional staff.

Lotteries

Local lotteries could provide an additional source of income for local authorities, albeit in competition with established forms of gambling, such as football pools, and other bodies, such as charities, which operate lotteries. However, the Lotteries Act 1975 empowered local authorities to promote lotteries for purposes for which they have power to incur expenditure. All proceeds, after deduction of expenses and prizes, have to be paid into a separate fund; expenditure financed by the fund will not rank for rate support grant. The limit of income from a lottery is £10 000 with a maximum of 52 lotteries per year, limiting the total maximum return to a local authority from this source to £520 000 per annum.

Although a variety of alternative sources of local authority income were explored in the White Paper,[15] no positive recommendations were made to pursue any of them actively.

Layfield Report and the Future in Local Government Finance

The Layfield Committee[16] was asked 'to review the whole system of local government finance' but its report in 1976 indicated that it found no system – only a collection of financial arrangements not properly related to each other and with obscure objectives. The Committee believed that responsibility must be firmly assigned to either central or local government, and preferred that councillors should be made more accountable for raising and spending money as the only way to sustain a vital local democracy. The Committee. also recommended that local authorities should be given greater powers of decision-making. Central government's control, which has been increasing despite expressed intentions to the contrary, should be limited to that necessary for national economic management.

The Committee generally supported the present rating system but advocated the abolition of precepting, so that every local authority would become a rating authority. A more fundamental recommendation is that the rating of domestic property should be based upon capital values (the customary assessment of the layman), with preparations for the introduction of capital value in England and Wales being put in hand as soon as possible, and with frequent revaluations. There is sufficient rental evidence available in Scotland for the present practice to continue there. The Royal Institution of Chartered Surveyors[17] strongly supports the capital value approach for domestic property.

The Layfield Committee urged a change in the method of assessing non-domestic property to direct net annual values; discontinuing the statutory deductions from gross value, and enabling the varying costs of repairs and maintenance to be reflected; and establishing a ratio between domestic and non-domestic property by applying a divisor to the domestic capital value to arrive at an 'assessed' value. This would also entail the abolition of domestic rate relief. The Royal Institution of Chartered Surveyors[17] considers that the use of a single divisor to convert all capital values to rateable values would be inequitable. The Institution suggests the use of more than one divisor throughout the range of capital values, and that, even then, there might be isolated cases of hardship where a ratepayer suffers a large increase in assessment after capital revaluation; this could be eased by a transitional arrangement to limit the increase of rates paid.

The Committee urged that where shopkeepers occupy living quarters attached to shops, the residential accommodation should not bear a heavier burden than other domestic property. Monthly instalments should become the normal method of payment for all ratepayers. Agricultural land and buildings should cease to be derated, although it was accepted that this might take five years to implement. The Report advocated changes in the appeals procedure to reduce the present strain on the machinery.

As to additional sources of income, the Committee favoured the introduction of local income tax levied by the major spending authorities. It would be based on the same rules and conventions as the national tax system and would be levied according to place of residence. It could be expressed as 'pence additional to national tax rates or as a percentage of national tax'.

As to grants in aid, the Committee believed that block grants are desirable but that they should play a smaller role with grant levels kept as low as possible. Some specific grants might also still be needed – for expenditure by only a few authorities, where costs vary widely, or for limited periods to finance new policies and new needs.

The main sources of borrowing have been and should remain the Public Works Loan Board, the domestic capital market and the foreign currency market. It is argued that the Public Works Loan Board should be regarded as a lender of last resort and that its charges should have a modestly penal character to encourage local authorities to satisfy their needs in the open market. This argument loses much of its substance when the 'last resort' caters for half the borrowing.[18] The Report warned against excessive temporary borrowing and stated that foreign currency borrowing has not been a regular and dependable source of finance. The Committee also believed that there was scope for financing a larger share of local government expenditure from charges.

The Report advocated the creation of a new forum to keep the financial relationship between the Government and local authorities under continuous review, and urged the establishment of an independent audit service in England and Wales.

A Government Green Paper in 1977 recommended the substitution of capital value domestic rate assessment for the largely hypothetical rental values, while admitting that this could not be implemented before 1982–3 and that it would place heavier burdens on occupiers of more expensive and cheaper properties. None of the other Layfield proposals was accepted. The Government also favoured a unitary grant system linked to individual local authorities' assessed spending needs.

References

1. HEPWORTH, N. P., *The Finance of Local Government* (Allen and Unwin, 1976).
2. JACKSON, P. W., *Local Government* (Butterworth, 1976).

3. RICHARDS, P. G., *The Reformed Local Government System* (Allen and Unwin, 1975).

4. LITTLE, B. St L., 'The effects of too much government grant', *Local Government Chronicle,* 9 April 1976.

5. CHARTERED INSTITUTE OF PUBLIC FINANCE AND ACCOUNTANCY, *Return of local authority outstanding debt for England and Wales as at 31 March 1975* (1976).

6. WHITE, J. H., 'Local authorities' important role in the money market', *The Building Societies Gazette,* January 1977.

7. CROSS, C. A., *Principles of Local Government Law* (Sweet and Maxwell, 1974).

8. HART, W. O. and GARNER, J. F., *Hart's Introduction to the Law of Local Government and Administration* (Butterworth, 1973).

9. ROYAL INSTITUTE OF PUBLIC ADMINISTRATION, *New sources of local revenue* (1956).

10. LITTLE, B. St L., 'From the specific to the general', *Local Government Chronicle,* 26 November 1976.

11. BUCKNALL, B., 'Metropolitan discontent', *Local Government Chronicle*, 18 June 1976.

12. ESTATES TIMES, 'High rates the biggest problem', *Estates Times*, 25 March 1977.

13. DOBSON, C., 'Few winners in rates explosion', *The Sunday Telegraph*, 6 February 1977.

14. FABIAN SOCIETY, Research series 295: *New revenues for local government* (1971).

15. Cmnd. 4741, *The future shape of local government finance* (H.M.S.O., 1971).

16. Cmnd. 6453, *Report of the Committee of Enquiry on Local Government Finance* – the Layfield Committee (H.M.S.O., 1976).

17. 'Memorandum of Observations by Royal Institution of Chartered Surveyors to the Department of the Environment. Local government finance: The Layfield Report', *The Chartered Surveyor*, March 1977.

18. MUNICIPAL AND PUBLIC SERVICES JOURNAL, 'A closer look at the Layfield Report', *Municipal and Public Services Journal*, 28 May 1976.

CHAPTER EIGHT

POWERS AND RESPONSIBILITIES OF LOCAL AUTHORITIES

General Powers

Local authorities derive a general framework of powers from the Local Government Act 1972, following the pattern previously established by the 1933 Act. Nevertheless constraints are placed upon local authorities in the way that they can act and they are limited to discharging duties and exercising powers conferred upon them by Acts of Parliament. Thus section 110 of the 1972 Act authorises local authorities to do anything 'which is calculated to facilitate, or is conducive or incidental to, the discharge of any of their functions'. This includes expenditure, borrowing or lending money, or acquiring or disposing of any property or rights. This power is however subject to the provisions of any relevant enactment and it does not in itself authorise raising money, whether by rate, precept or borrowing, or lending money, except in accordance with the appropriate enactments.[1]

The Act preserves the fundamental principle that Parliament alone authorises local authorities to take specific action – the Act providing the machinery but the Government retaining the power to operate it.

Statutory Instruments

Many general Acts confer upon Ministers the power to make Rules, Orders and Regulations (Statutory Instruments) which may control the activities of local authorities or conversely provide them with greater authority. These Statutory Instruments serve three principal functions.

1. To provide flexible administration.
2. To secure uniformity.
3. To relieve pressure on the parliamentary timetable.

The large size and very full timetable of Parliament generally restricts its activities to the formulation of broad principles and policies. Furthermore, the passing of amending Bills is generally a lengthy process. Regulations, on the other hand, can be made and annulled quite quickly. Hence it is customary to leave most matters of administrative detail to be determined by Ministers through Regulations, and these are sometimes referred to as delegated legislation.

There are some restrictions on the operation of Statutory Instruments.

1. They can only be made under statutory authority and within the limits of that authority.
2. Courts of Law may declare them *ultra vires* if they extend outside the statutory authority.
3. Some of them cannot operate until they have been approved by resolution of both Houses of Parliament.

Doctrine of Ultra Vires

Ultra vires is an important doctrine in local government administration and means acting beyond the powers. An individual may do anything which is not prohibited by law whereas a local authority is only permitted to do those things which are authorised by law. These powers as previously shown are detailed in various statutes relating to local government. For instance, metropolitan district councils can provide education and social services, but non-metropolitan district councils do not have this power as the Local Government Act 1972 restricts these functions to non-metropolitan county councils. Local authorities must keep within their legal powers and exercise their functions in a reasonable manner.

There are a number of possible legal consequences which may flow from a failure by a local authority to observe the *ultra vires* doctrine. For example, an *ultra vires* contract cannot be enforced in the courts, and anyone prejudiced can take action for damages or apply to the High Court for an injunction to restrain the local authority from acting or continuing to act beyond its powers. Any expenditure in an *ultra vires* action is illegal and the district auditor has a duty to disallow the amount and to surcharge the persons responsible for incurring it. It is also a good defence to a prosecution for an offence under a bye-law to show that it is *ultra vires*.[2]

There are many cases invoking the operation of this doctrine and a few will serve to illustrate their general nature. In *Attorney-General* v. *Fulham Corporation* (1921) the court held that the local authority's powers under the Baths and Washhouses Acts 1846–78 did not include the power to operate a municipal laundry. In *Prescott* v. *Birmingham Corporation* (1955) the provision of free bus travel to old-age pensioners in the absence of statutory authority was held to be *ultra vires*.[2]

The Local Government Act 1972 slightly relaxes the *ultra vires* rule by authorising local authorities to do 'anything which is calculated to facilitate, or is conducive or incidental to, the discharge of their functions'. The Maud Committee[3] considered that the *ultra vires* doctrine operated to the disadvantage of local government because it discouraged enterprise, handicapped development, robbed the community of services which local government might provide and encouraged too much central government control. The committee recommended that its impact be reduced by the following.

1. Enabling local authorities to do whatever in their opinion is in the interests of the inhabitants, subject to certain safeguards such as avoiding encroachment on the powers of other bodies.
2. Removing statutory regulation of the manner in which local authorities perform their functions.
3. Abolishing the district auditor's power of surcharge.

There is a general requirement on local authorities to observe certain rules of equitable behaviour known as the principles of natural justice. The two most important rules are that no man may be judge in his own cause and that no man may be condemned unheard.[4]

In the first case bias may arise from a local authority member having a pecuniary or other interest in the matter being decided, resulting in a likelihood of partiality being present.[1] A good example was the quashing of the decision of Hendon Rural District Council in 1933 to approve the erection of a roadhouse because one of the councillors involved had a financial interest in the proposed development.[4]

For judicial proceedings to be valid, a party must be given adequate notice of the case against him and an opportunity to be heard in his defence, with the judge hearing both sides on an equal basis.[1] This rule has particular significance in the conduct of public inquiries into local authority proposals, many of which affect private property. Appropriate examples include *Broadbent* v. *Rotherham Corporation* (1917),[1] where the local authority made a demolition order in respect of certain unfit premises without considering the plaintiff's application to undertake essential repairs, and *Errington* v. *Ministry of Health* (1935),[4] where a Ministry inspector visited a clearance order site without permitting the objectors to be present.

Judicial Control

The courts have jurisdiction over local authorities in various ways.

1. *Actions for an injunction or declaration* An injunction is an order
of court requiring a local authority to restrain from the performance
of a specific act, such as where the members of a local authority
were threatened by a judge with committal to prison for contempt
of court because the local authority had failed to comply with
an injunction to stop discharging untreated sewage into a river.

Where the aggrieved persons consist of the general body of ratepayers, the action is normally taken on their behalf by the Attorney-
General, while if individuals only are affected they usually conduct
their own case.

2. *Order of mandamus* This is an order made by the court requiring
a local authority to perform a particular duty which it has neglected
or refused to do. It cannot however be compelled to perform a
discretionary function.

3. *Statutory appeals* Many of the powers conferred on local authorities
by statute affect the private interests of individuals and hence a safeguard is provided in the form of a right of appeal against the
improper or inequitable use of the powers. The appeals
arrangements are now outlined.

(i) Appeals to the local justices in Courts of Summary Jurisdiction
are provided for in many statutes. A typical example is the
Highways Act 1959, whereby owners of properties abutting
private streets may object to the specification of works served
upon them for making up, paving and draining the street.
There is also a right of appeal to the justices against the refusal
of local authorities to grant licences for conducting certain
businesses. Appeals can sometimes be made to county justices
in County Courts, as for instance under the Public Health Act
1925 against orders of local authorities declaring existing
highways to be new streets.

(ii) Appeals to the County Court provide another alternative route
of appeal. For example, the Housing Act 1957 gives property
owners a right of appeal to a local County Court against
demolition, closing and similar orders.

(iii) Appeals to the High Court can be made for the purposes
described earlier in the chapter. Additionally, many statutes
provide a right of appeal to the High Court against orders
made by local authorities and confirmed by Ministers of the
Crown. Typical examples include clearance and compulsory
purchase orders made under the Housing Act 1957. In these
instances a time limit is prescribed for the exercise of the right

of appeal (within six weeks of confirmation of order) and the High Court can only quash the order if it is made *ultra vires* or does not comply with some statutory requirement.

Hart[1] has described how the courts of law must accept as valid the legal powers which the statute has granted, and are confined to deciding particular cases where it is alleged that these powers have been exceeded. They cannot thus exercise any effective control over the manner in which statutory powers are used and are unable to supervise either the details of administration or the framing of policy within the limits prescribed by statute.

Acts of Parliament

Acts of Parliament form the most effective and direct method of conferring powers on local authorities. Although there is much delegated legislation, this does not undermine the fundamental principle that the powers of local authorities must be derived from Parliament; it merely introduces a two-stage process. Acts of Parliament affecting local authority activities may take several forms: public or general Acts; private or local Acts; and Clauses Acts.

Public Acts

Public or general Acts confer most powers of local authorities; some, like the Education Act 1944 and the Town and Country Planning Act 1971, set up or regulate the administration of a complete local government service. These statutes remain in force until repealed or amended by subsequent legislation and there are hundreds of Acts which impose duties or confer powers on local authorities. Public Acts have general application, form part of the general law of the land and operate countrywide.

These Acts follow the normal parliamentary procedure in order to obtain approval. Each receives formal first and second readings in the House of Commons to secure approval to the general principle, and then passes to a select or standing committee for important or controversial measures, to a committee of the whole House, where it is considered clause by clause, and on completion the Bill is reported to the House. The Bill is read a third time and then sent up to the House of Lords, where it passes through similar processes. Finally the Bill receives Royal Assent and becomes an Act of Parliament.

Such Acts may be *obligatory* in their terms by compelling local authorities to exercise the powers they confer. This approach is particularly suited to Acts introducing new services throughout the country. Alternatively Acts may be *permissive*, giving local authorities discretion in the exercise of the particular functions. A third approach is *adoptive* Acts, whereby the powers operate only where the local authority takes the prescribed action to adopt the Act, thus providing flexibility and scope for innovation. For example, many of the provisions of the Public Health Acts of 1890, 1907 and 1925 were adoptive but they were later embodied in the 1936 Act as permissive powers.[1]

Private Acts

Private or local Acts are passed by Parliament on the petition of a person or body, conferring special powers on a particular matter or in a particular locality. Most of the larger local authorities have powers derived in this way and the Local Government Act 1972 enables these arrangements to continue. Parliament is thus able to confer legal powers on all local authorities in general and also to one authority in particular to meet its special needs.

Any local authority has the power to promote or oppose a private or local Bill in Parliament following the prescribed procedure. A resolution must be passed by a majority of all members of the authority at a meeting summoned after 30 days' notice for promotion of a Bill or ten days' notice where a Bill is to be opposed, including the giving of notice in the local press. The resolution must be published in the local press and a copy sent to the appropriate Minister. The local authority must confirm the resolution in a similar manner after the Bill has been deposited in Parliament.

The parliamentary procedure for private Bills is governed by the Standing Orders of each House and these ensure that the sovereignty of Parliament is not employed in the interests of any individual or body without adequate opportunity given to any affected persons to oppose the measure.[1] These Standing Orders require draft private Bills to be deposited in both Houses and to be inspected by examiners, with copies sent to appropriate government departments. The subsequent passage of the Bill bears some resemblance to that of a public Bill. The first reading is formal and so often is the second, although an objection can be made at this stage. Most of the work is carried out at the committee stage, where the promoters and opponents of the Bill represented by counsel appear before the committee and call witnesses, dealing with the Bill clause by clause. Hart[1] has described how the committee not only weighs the benefits to be derived by the promoters against the public interest involved, but also holds the scale of justice as between the promoters and other private interests. At the report stage, the Bill with any amendments is reported to the House and the third formal reading takes place. The Bill passes through similar processes in the other House and, if approved, receives the Royal Assent and becomes law.[2]

Clauses Acts

Private Bill procedure is both lengthy and costly and during the 1840s Parliament passed a number of Clauses Acts containing groups of clauses modelled on those which had previously appeared in local Acts. Many of these clauses related to local government activities such as cemeteries, gasworks, markets and fairs, harbours, town police, town improvements, and waterworks.[1] Private Bills formulated subsequently could thus incorporate the appropriate clauses and so reduce both the time and cost of the detailed examination of the Bill by the parliamentary committee. The committee has primarily to decide whether the local authority should be permitted to provide the particular service and whether the modifications of the Clauses Acts requested to suit local conditions are acceptable.

Local authorities will continue to use the private Bill procedure to obtain additional powers outside the scope of general legislation, but the Clauses Acts provide a speedier and more uniform approach. Some of the Clauses Acts have since been embodied in public Acts of general application as, for example, the replacement of the Waterworks Clauses Acts by the Water Act 1945.

Orders

Provisional Orders were introduced to save local authorities the expense of private legislation. Various public Acts enable local authorities to obtain additional powers by Provisional Orders made by the appropriate Minister and confirmed by Parliament, and the procedure has now been regularised in the Local Government Act 1972 (Section 240). The Minister may, if he thinks fit, refuse to act. Where he considers the matter further, the proposal is publicised in the *London Gazette* and the local press. Objections of interested parties are considered by the Minister, who will generally order the holding of a local inquiry before a Ministry inspector, who hears the evidence and objections. The inspector reports to the Minister, who then decides the application. If the Minister supports the application, he makes a Provisional Order which requires confirmation by Parliament through a Provisional Orders Confirmation Bill. The Order is thus processed through Parliament as a

Government measure and, unless opponents petition against the Order, it will obtain the force of law in a relatively short period of time.[1]

Three conditions have to be met.

1. A Minister or Government department must have a statutory power to make Provisional Orders of the type proposed.
2. The local authority must apply to the appropriate Minister or department and comply with the publicity requirements.
3. The Order has no force until confirmed by Parliament.[1]

The Statutory Orders (Special Procedure) Acts 1945 and 1965 introduced *Special Parliamentary Procedure Orders*, which simplify the Provisional Order procedure and have in many instances been substituted for it. The Order is made by the appropriate Minister, notice is given in the press and a public inquiry is held if there are objections. The Order is submitted to Parliament and either House may annul it by resolution within fourteen days. If it is not annulled and no petitions are submitted, the Order takes effect. Otherwise it passes to a joint committee of both Houses. If the joint committee amends the Order, the Minister may accept the amended Order, withdraw the Order or submit the original proposals in the form of a public Bill. Otherwise the Order becomes effective on approval by the committee. This procedure is quicker and cheaper than a private Bill or Provisional Order and is particularly suitable for non-contentious matters, but there must be provision in the appropriate Act for the use of this procedure.[2]

Bye-laws

Nature and Scope

Bye-laws are subordinate legislation in the form of local laws, affecting the public or a section of the public within an area, and are enforceable in the ordinary courts. Lord Russell C.J. gave a definition in *Kruse* v. *Johnson* (1898): 'A bye-law . . . I take to be an ordinance affecting the public, or some portion of the public, imposed by some authority clothed with statutory powers ordering something to be done or not to be done, and accompanied by some sanction or penalty for its non-observance. It necessarily involves restriction of liberty of action by persons who come under its operation as to acts which, but for the bye-law, they would be free to do or not to do as they please. Further, it involves this consequence – that, if validly made, it has the force of law within the sphere of its legitimate operation.'

Hart[1] considers this definition to be too wide as it would embrace, for instance, some of the delegated legislation stemming from Government departments, whereas the application of the term is being confined here to local government. In this latter context bye-laws have the following characteristics.

1. They are local laws affecting all persons within their area of operation and are enforceable in the courts by the imposition of a penalty.
2. Power to make them must be derived from statute.
3. Ordinary courts have the right to review them and to determine whether or not they have been validly made.

Cross[5] has listed the large number of statutes which authorise the making of bye-laws relating to local authority functions. The range of subjects is very wide indeed and includes allotments, burials and cremation, children and young persons, food and drugs, highways, libraries and museums, parks, recreational facilities and open spaces, housing, public health, water supply, and weights and measures.

Making of Bye-laws

Prior to the Local Government Act 1933 there were three classes of bye-laws.

1. Bye laws for the good rule and government of the areas of boroughs and counties.
2. Sanitary bye-laws for the prevention and suppression of nuisances made by borough and county councils.
3. Other bye-laws derived from statutes setting up or regulating particular local authority services.[1]

The Local Government Act 1933 aimed at providing a uniform code for making bye-laws, as far as practicable, without fundamentally affecting the provisions and objectives of the enactments from which the powers were obtained. The Local Government Act 1972 has further simplified the powers and procedure for making and confirming bye-laws.

The 1972 Act removed the differences between bye-laws for good rule and government and those for the prevention and suppression of nuisances, by conferring on all district councils the power to make both types of bye-laws and providing that all these bye-laws require confirmation by the Minister. Nevertheless, various statutes confer the power to make bye-laws for particular services on the different types of local authority, ranging from county councils to parish councils.

The procedure prescribed in the 1972 Act for the making and confirmation of bye-laws applies to all bye-laws made by local authorities under any enactments which do not prescribe any other procedure. This Act further provides for bye-laws to be made under the common seal of the local authority, except in the case of parish and community councils which do not have a seal, where they can be made under the hands and seals of two members of the council. One month's notice of a local authority's intention to apply for confirmation of bye-laws must be given in the local press, and throughout that period a copy of the bye-laws must be available for public inspection at the authority's offices. The bye-laws cannot operate until confirmed.

Confirmation of Bye-laws

The Local Government Act 1972 prescribes that the confirming authority is the authority or person listed in the enactment under which the bye-laws are made. For example, the Food and Drugs Act 1955 names the Minister of Agriculture, Fisheries and Food as the confirming authority for bye-laws relating to slaughterhouses and knackers' yards. Where the particular enactment does not prescribe the confirming authority, then it shall be the Secretary of State.

Following confirmation, bye-laws shall be printed and copies made available for public inspection and purchase at the local authority offices. Copies of district council bye-laws must be sent to the county council and the parish or community councils, or the chairman of the parish meeting where there is no parish council, in whose areas they apply. County council bye-laws must be sent to every district council in the county.

Model Bye-laws

If each local authority made its own bye-laws in isolation there could be wide variations in their objectives and approach. In practice a considerable measure of uniformity is achieved without complete loss of flexibility. The uniformity is obtained through central government scrutiny and approval, bearing in mind that many of the problems facing local government throughout the country have similar characteristics and usually respond to like solutions.

Government departments have also made a practice of issuing sets of model bye-laws to provide guidelines to local authorities in formulating their own bye-laws. Local authorities are not compelled to adopt the model bye-laws, but would be wise to follow them unless there are exceptional circumstances calling for a different approach. The submission of bye-laws based on the model bye-laws is likely to quicken their confirmation. Furthermore, model bye-laws are often based on experience gained in different parts of the country and, on occasions, the validity of their provisions has been tested in the courts.

Validity of Bye-laws

Bye-laws are not operable until they have been ratified in the manner previously described. Unlike statutes, bye-laws are subject to scrutiny by the courts. For example, the statutes giving powers to make bye-laws authorise the imposition of a penalty, usually not exceeding £20, for their infringement, and provide for the recovery of this penalty in a summary manner. It is open to a person prosecuted for breach of a bye-law to argue that the bye-law itself is invalid in that it has not been properly made or that it is *ultra vires*.[1]

A number of judicial tests have been established to determine the validity of bye-laws and these are now considered.

1. *Reasonableness* This is difficult to define and Lord Russell in *Kruse* v. *Johnson* (1898) stated that 'a bye-law is not unreasonable merely because particular judges may think that it goes further than is prudent or necessary or convenient'.

In *Parker* v. *Bournemouth Corporation* (1902) a power to make bye-laws for regulating the selling or hawking of any article on a beach or foreshore was held to be unreasonably exercised by a bye-law providing that 'a person shall not on the said beach or foreshore sell or hawk or offer or expose for sale any article, commodity, or thing, except in pursuance of an agreement with the corporation'. It withdrew from the courts the question of reasonableness, by making the corporation the sole judge of the reasonableness of any agreement it chose to make, and went still further by providing for any person to be prohibited altogether from selling.[1]

2. *Certainty of terms* A bye-law must be certain and thus contain adequate information as to the duties of those who are to comply with it. Thus a bye-law for 'good rule and government' which provided that 'no person shall wilfully annoy passengers in the street' was held to be too uncertain and therefore void in *Nash* v. *Finlay* (1901).

3. *Consistency with the general law* A bye-law is invalid if it is inconsistent with or repugnant to the general law, or if it relates to matters already adequately covered by statute law. In *Powell* v. *May* (1946)

a bye-law made by Glamorgan County Council prohibited betting in a public place, despite the fact that both the Street Betting Act 1906 and the Betting and Lotteries Act 1934 allowed betting in a public place subject to compliance with certain requirements. It was held that the bye-law was bad, for it prohibited the doing of an act which the law expressly or implicitly allowed.[5]

4. *Intra vires* A bye-law must be within the scope of the statutory power under which it is made. In *R.* v. *Wood* (1855) the Public Health Act 1848 enabled a local board of health to make bye-laws relating to the removal by the occupier of dust, ashes, rubbish, filth, manure, dung and soil. A local board made a bye-law under this enactment directing all occupiers to remove all snow from the footpath opposite their premises. It was held that the bye-law was *ultra vires*, since it went beyond the enabling powers.[5]

Relaxation and Re-approval of Bye-laws

A local authority has no power to waive or relax its bye-laws unless there is a specific enabling statutory provision or, as is very unlikely, the bye-laws themselves contain such a provision. The Highways Act 1959 and the Water Act 1945 are examples of Acts containing relaxation provisions, in respect of new street bye-laws and bye-laws for preventing waste of water respectively.

The Public Health Act 1936 introduced a new principle to keep some of the bye-laws authorised under the Act compatible with current conditions by requiring review at ten-yearly intervals.

Legal Status of Local Authorities

Local authorities are corporate bodies and as such they are legal entities each composed of a number of individuals, which the law regards as a single body with a legal existence separate from the individuals who make up the corporation. A corporation has perpetual succession irrespective of its changing membership. It has a seal for use with the more important formal acts, although the Corporate Bodies' Contracts Act 1960 has considerably reduced the number of instances where a seal is used. Local authorities as corporations can sue and be sued and hold property in their own name.[2]

Local Authorities in Litigation

Local authorities cannot plead the performance of their public duties as a defence to actions in tort as, like trading corporations, they are liable for damages and may be restrained by injunction.

Since local authorities are corporations, they can act only through the agency of others. Nevertheless a statutory corporation may be liable in damages for torts (civil wrongs) committed by its servants. For example, a teacher appointed by a local education authority is a servant, and this will impose liability on the authority for injuries negligently caused by him to a pupil.

Where a statute provides that a local authority may or must do an act which would otherwise be tortious, the act cannot be actionable. However the statute requires careful analysis because, if the limits prescribed by the Act are exceeded, the act will be illegal. For example, a statute authorising the erection of a small-pox hospital provides no defence to an authority building it in such a position as to cause a nuisance to private individuals.[1]

A local authority has a duty to exercise reasonable care when performing its functions. The performance of obligatory duties are enforceable by public proceedings, often by an order of mandamus.

In general an action for failure to perform a statutory duty will only be available where the statute confers a right of action upon the plaintiff, either as a specific individual or as a member of a group for whose benefit the provision was made. Notwithstanding this, if a duty owed to the public at large is carried out carelessly resulting in injury to an individual, he may sue for damages in an action in negligence. For example, in *Dutton* v. *Bognor Regis United Building Co Ltd* (1972), the Court of Appeal held a local authority liable in tort to a purchaser from the original owner of a house which subsided because of insecure foundations some years after erection. The house had been inspected and approved by the local authority's building inspector under building bye-laws. As the inspector had been careless in his inspection, the local authority was held liable.

Prior to 1964 highway authorities were not liable for non-feasance and hence were not liable in a civil action to a member of the public injured through their failure to maintain their roads in proper repair. They have always been liable for mis-feasance as instanced by dangerous conditions resulting from road repairs. The Highways (Miscellaneous Provisions) Act 1961 abrogated the exemption for the non-repair rule as from 1 August 1964. It is however a defence for a highway authority to show that it had taken reasonable care to ensure that the highway was not dangerous for traffic.[1]

Commissioners for Local Administration

The Local Government Act 1974 established two commissions for local administration, one for England and the other for Wales, each embodying parliamentary and local commissioners. The commissions make the necessary administrative arrangements including appointing staff, providing accommodation and publishing information about the procedure for making complaints. The commissioners investigate the complaints. The Act also provides for two representative bodies, one for England and the other for Wales, consisting of representatives of the bodies subject to investigation by the local commissioners – that is, local authorities (excluding parish and community councils), water authorities, joint boards and police authorities.

The acts of committees, of members, of officers and of the authority itself may be investigated. But the following matters are excluded from investigation.

1. Where a complainant has or had a right of appeal to a tribunal or a Minister or by way of legal proceedings.

2. An act which affects all or most of the inhabitants of the area.

3. A complaint about anything done before 1 April 1974.

4. A complaint about action taken in matters relating to contractual or other commercial transactions.

5. Action taken in personnel matters – appointments, removals, pay, discipline and the like.

6. Certain actions taken in the education service, including the giving of instruction, and the conduct, curriculum and internal management of schools.

A complaint may be made by an individual or a body of persons concerning alleged maladministration. Complaints are made in writing to a member of the authority concerned and must specify the action alleged to constitute maladministration. The reason for requiring a complaint to go through a member is to emphasise the role of the elected member in redressing grievances. If the member refuses to pass the complaint on to the commissioner, the commissioner can receive the complaint direct from the complainant. The complaint must be made to the member within twelve months of the day on which the complainant first had notice of the matters alleged. This can be waived but will probably be only for very strong reasons, such as illness.[6]

The first annual report of the Commissioners for Local Administration in England[7] covers the period up to 31 March 1976. The numbers of complaints received and investigated are as follows:

complaints not acceptable for investigation	1749
complaints where investigation revealed maladministration and injustice	49
complaints where investigation revealed maladministration but no injustice	3
complaints where investigation revealed no maladministration	47
complaints still under consideration	401
total	2249

The rejection of 1749 complaints as not acceptable stems from the fact that they were outside the commission's jurisdiction. As many as 783 complaints were not acceptable because the complainant could not point to any specific act of maladministration or injustice; most of these complaints were about the merits of a decision or action and not about the manner in which it was made or taken.

One of the commission's main difficulties is that many complainants are unskilled in self-expression, whether in writing or by word of mouth. This results in a considerable amount of time being taken by the commission's staff in ascertaining the true nature of the problem and conveying it in comprehensible terms to the authority, so that it may check the facts and offer its comments.

When the grounds of complaint are unravelled many prove to be capable of a simple solution or remedy: what appeared to be maladministration to an aggrieved person may turn out to be a simple misunderstanding of what they wanted or did not want.

The report[7] distinguishes two stages in handling complaints – the informal inquiry and the formal investigation. So many difficulties can be removed by a chat with council officials, then if the matter can be cleared up to the satisfaction of the complainant, this is done without further proceedings. When the commission finds insufficient or no grounds for a formal investigation, the reasons are given to the complainant; if alternative courses of action seem likely to prove useful they are suggested.

When a formal investigation is completed, the local commissioner sends his report to the complainant, to the authority and to the member who referred the complaint. The authority is asked to state what action it has taken or intends to take when maladministration has been found. The commissions do not propose remedies but are prepared to comment on suggested remedies proposed by authorities.

The remedies normally appropriate are stated in the report[7] to fall into two broad categories.

1. Steps to prevent the recurrence of similar maladministration.
2. Direct removal of the grievance – for example, by remedying a planning error, arranging a housing transfer, or compensating the complainant by an *ex gratia* payment.

The commission comments that its work would be in vain if practices and procedures were not improved as a result of its investigations.

Complaints investigated where maladministration has been revealed cover a wide range of local authority functions, and a few reported decisions will serve to illustrate this.

1. Failure to provide an opportunity to make representations against a planning application, and undue bias shown in favour of the applicant.
2. Unnecessary concern and worry caused by misleading information about plans for the compulsory purchase of houses.
3. Abuse of planning procedures in granting permission for building a bungalow.
4. Unfairness arising out of the way in which 11-plus selection and appeals procedures were carried out.
5. Decision, taken on wrong facts, not to hold an inquiry into complaint about relationship between a headmaster and his 18-year-old head girl.
6. Delays and failures by council following discovery of rat-infested council houses and over consequent moves to alternative homes.

One of the main criticisms of the procedure is that the commissions have no power over local authorities – the safeguard consists of an impartial investigation followed by publicity. Some feel that maladministration may be difficult to define although the published reports mainly centre around improper and inadequate action. More formal lodging of complaints has been suggested as a method of extending the commission's usefulness.[8]

The report of the first year's work of the commission has shown the extent of maladministration in English local government to be small. There is little doubt that the commission has helped considerably in removing doubts in the public's mind about possible extensive maladministration in the local government service and in providing an effective complaint machinery.

References

1. HART, W. O. and GARNER, J. F., *Hart's Introduction to the Law of Local Government Administration* (Butterworth, 1973).
2. CLARKE, H. W., *Administrative Law for Surveying Students* (Sweet and Maxwell, 1970).

3. *Report of the Committee on the Management of Local Government* – the Maud Report (H.M.S.O., 1967).
4. RICHARDS, P. G., *The Reformed Local Government System* (Allen and Unwin, 1975).
5. CROSS, C. A., *Principles of Local Government Law* (Sweet and Maxwell, 1974).
6. FOULKES, D., 'The local ombudsman', *Local Government Chronicle*, 25 July 1975.
7. *The First Annual Report of the Commissioners for Local Administration in England* (H.M.S.O., 1976).
8. LOCAL GOVERNMENT REVIEW, 'The voice of local government', *Local Government Review*, 2 October 1976.

CHAPTER NINE

CENTRAL GOVERNMENT CONTROL

Central and Local Government Relationships

There was little central control of local government before 1830, apart from an indiscriminate and unco-ordinated form of judicial control. The courts took action only after difficulties occurred and these arrangements militated against the implementation of central policy and the control of expenditure. The need to secure uniformity of poor law administration countrywide resulted in the establishment of the Poor Law Commissioners and the forging of the present central–local relationships.

Jackson[1] has shown how no local authority can be completely autonomous and how all are dependent upon central government for the conferment of powers, as described in Chapter 8. Parliament decides the functions of local authorities and gives them wide discretion in certain directions. The effective administration of some local services, such as education, police and public health, is essential to the welfare of the country as a whole, and central government is justifiably anxious to maintain prescribed minimum standards of service. Having achieved these minimum standards local authorities are free to develop and vary the scope of the services to meet local needs within the national framework. Central control of the permissive functions of local authorities, such as the provision of council offices, will be less exacting.

Within these limitations local authorities can exercise a considerable degree of discretion, and this freedom of action is essential if local government is to operate effectively in meeting local needs. If all local decision-making were to be dominated by central government, it would cease to be local government and become merely an agent of central government. Nevertheless as Hart[2] has described, local wishes to experiment or to reduce burdens may at times conflict with a justifiable central wish for some uniformity and equality of service.

Central government departments have no legal control of the work other than that directly conferred by statute. The control is however mainly exercised informally through a process of consultation between local authorities and officers of the various Government departments or Ministries and in the issue of circulars and memoranda. In this way Government departmental policy pervades the work of local authorities, described by Cross[3] as 'government by circular'.

Some have suggested that the central–local government relationship is a partnership, while others identify a principal/agent arrangement. Richards[4] has described how central government needs the co-operation of local authorities and information from them on local conditions, problems and needs, and local authorities, for their part, often require central government help and advice. At the same time local authorities depend for their powers on national legislation and some local government law is framed on the principal/agent concept – the education and social services being good examples.

In practice, four distinct forms of central control of local authorities can be identified.

1. Legislative control by Parliament.
2. Administrative control by Government departments.
3. Financial control by Government departments.
4. Judicial control by the courts, as described in Chapter 8.

The main reasons for central control are as follows.

1. The importance of the work of local authorities in the public sector of the national economy and the resultant need to ensure that local authority expenditure is consistent with the Government's general economic policy.
2. The high proportion of local authority income by way of Government grant and Parliament's wish to exercise some supervision over the spending of this money.
3. The national importance of much of the work of local authorities and the recent tendency to require certain minimum standards of provision.
4. The need to protect ratepayers against possible financial mismanagement by local authorities, by means of Government loan sanction and audit.
5. The desirability of protecting local authority staff against arbitrary dismissal.
6. The need to provide suitable machinery for the settlement of disputes between the local authority and individuals, particularly with regard to alleged maladministration through local commissioners as described in Chapter 8.

Legislative Control

Although local authorities are legally independent bodies with powers and duties derived directly from Acts of Parliament, they are subject to a substantial measure of control by Ministers and central government departments, mainly based on statute.[5] Some Acts of Parliament vest a supervisory power in a Minister of the Crown. For example, the Education Act 1944 places a duty on the Secretary of State for Education and Science 'to promote the education of the people of England and Wales and the progressive development of institutions devoted to that purpose, and to secure the effective execution by local authorities, under his control and direction, of the national policy for providing a varied and comprehensive educational service in every area'. In addition to these general powers there are many statutes giving varying degrees of central administrative control over local authorities.

It is important to realise that local authorities require statutory powers to enable them to engage in almost any activity which they wish to undertake. Parliament in its law-making capacity is able to confer or refuse these powers and hence exercises control over the development and activities of local government.[2]

There are three main reasons why local authorities require statutory powers to enable them to carry out their functions.

1. Local authorities need to raise money by rates to finance their activities and rates are a form of local tax which can be authorised only by Parliament.
2. Most of the services provided by local authorities involve interference with the rights of individuals, such as owners of compulsorily-acquired properties, and local authorities cannot interfere with these rights in the absence of statutory authority.
3. Local authorities are corporate bodies with a separate name, perpetual succession and a common seal, and in the eyes of the law a body corporate is a person. Local authorities are statutorily-created bodies (statutory corporations) and thus can perform only acts authorised by legislation. If they perform any acts outside these powers they will be acting *ultra vires*, as described in Chapter 8. Nevertheless it should be noted that the Local Government Act 1972 gives local authorities power to do anything which is calculated to facilitate, or which is conducive or incidental to, the discharge of any of their functions, even if they have no specific statutory power for that action.

Chapter 8 showed how local authorities derived their powers from Parliament in a variety of ways, ranging through Acts of Parliament, both public and private, provisional orders, statutory orders subject to special parliamentary procedure, and delegated legislation.

Under the last heading many general Acts confer upon Ministers the power to make Rules, Orders and Regulations, known collectively as Statutory Instruments. These rules and regulations provide a means of controlling the activities of local authorities although, on occasions, they give authorities greater powers.

Richards[4] has shown how local government law is complex, partly because of its detailed nature and partly because of the variety of forms of legal power. Some statutory authority emanates from the general Acts establishing particular types of local authority, such as the Local Government Act 1972 and the London Government Act 1963. Many powers derive from general Acts relating to specific local government functions such as the Education, Highways, Public Health and Town and Country Planning Acts. Furthermore, most of the duties conferred on local authorities are mandatory or compulsory, although with a few activities of lesser importance authorities have the choice of adopting the powers. An example of the latter category of power is the provision for the rating of unoccupied properties under the Local Government Acts 1966 and 1974.

The private Bill procedure, as described in Chapter 8, if used extensively could have widened considerably the scope of local government activities. Even with the simplification of the procedure for promotion of private Bills contained in the Local Government Act 1972, it is a lengthy, costly and complicated process.

It has become increasingly common for central government to discuss, with local authorities or their associations, draft legislation affecting local government. The views of the authorities which will be concerned with the administration of the legislation must be helpful to the Minister, and it also gives him the opportunity to explain the Government's thinking on the proposals to the local authority representatives, thus making for closer and more sympathetic working relationships. It also enables highly desirable amendments to be made to the draft legislation at an early stage, thus in all probability saving time later in the law-making process.[1]

Administrative Control

General Powers

The Poor Law Amendment Act 1834 introduced the first form of central control of local administration by a Government department. Hart[2] has described how administrative control by Government departments over not only the details of routine action, but also the formulation and implementation of policy, has expanded until it has become a characteristic feature of local government in England and Wales. In some cases it has even penetrated areas previously reserved to the courts. Indeed many activities of local authorities need approval by the appropriate Minister before they can be implemented. For example, bye-laws made by local authorities regulating the conduct of certain matters or use of facilities in their area become operative only when approved by the appropriate Minister. In like manner where a local education authority resolves to erect a school, the plans require approval by the Secretary of State for Education and Science.

Directions

Some statutes confer on government departments specific powers to issue directions to local authorities amounting to detailed administrative instructions on how they should exercise their powers. For example, the Town and Country Planning Act 1971 empowers the Minister to direct a planning authority to serve certain notices or to make certain orders authorised by the Act. If the planning authority fails to comply with these directions, the Minister may exercise the powers.[2]

Regulations

Statutes conferring powers or duties on local authorities often authorise a Minister to make regulations prescribing how particular functions shall be performed, the standards which a service shall satisfy or the conditions on which a grant is payable. The statute prescribes the broad principles relating to the power or duty, while the Minister often determines the detailed working arrangements. A typical example is the Town and Country Planning Act 1971, in which the Minister is given power to make regulations describing the way in which the Act is to be administered.[3]

Bye-laws

It was shown in Chapter 8 that local bye-laws cannot become effective until confirmed by the appropriate Minister, thus ensuring central control. The Government department in practice examines proposed bye-laws to ensure validity in law, and to satisfy itself that the need exists in the particular locality for the bye-law proposed, and that an attempt is made through the use of model codes to secure a reasonable measure of uniformity.[3]

Supervision

Government departments undertake supervision of the work of local authorities, with the extent of the supervision varying between functions and even between parts of functions. Central government is particularly concerned, for example, with major activities in education, police and town and country planning, but it is far less interested in such aspects as the provision of public libraries, municipal entertainments and recreational facilities. Similarly, the Department of the Environment is very much concerned with the amount and type of local authority house-building, and the standards of design and construction and costs, while leaving the local authority free to select tenants by whatever method it chooses. Central government is very much involved with major road proposals and improvements, but does not concern itself with the maintenance of minor roads. Most of the supervisory functions of central government are specifically authorised by statute, but there are some cases where Ministers carry out a broad surveillance of a particular local authority function.[4] Some Acts give Ministers a reserve or default power over local authorities, as described later in the chapter.

Inspection

Ministers who have the statutory duty of supervising local authority services generally appoint inspectors or other officers to keep the services under review and to provide a means of contact with the local authorities.[1] An inspector ensures that local authority services are efficient and that standards are maintained, and he also advises local authorities and his own department on both policy and technique aspects. Police, fire, education and children services are subject to regular inspection.[4] The Department of the Environment employs a large inspectorate but these are primarily engaged on the conduct of local inquiries and informal hearings into planning appeals, objections to compulsory purchase orders, and capital schemes.

Other Ministerial Actions and Requirements

Local authorities are required to obtain ministerial approval for their administrative arrangements for certain services, such as fire and welfare. Ministers may also prepare schemes for the formation of joint boards to undertake specific functions, such as fire and police. Local authorities have a general power to form joint committees, but this can be exercised only in relation to certain services, such as education and fire, with the approval of the appropriate Minister.[4]

Various statutes require local authorities to make annual returns to the supervising department, such as annual reports under the

Offices, Shops and Railway Premises Act 1963. Many other returns are required by Ministers under administrative procedures quite apart from any statutory requirements, while, as described in Chapter 4, the appointments of certain statutory officers responsible for important services are subject to the approval of the appropriate Minister, and ministerial sanction is also required for their dismissal in certain cases. This latter requirement aims at encouraging freedom of action by chief officers in carrying out statutory duties in the face of local pressures.[3]

Local authorities can exercise their powers in certain matters only with the prior approval of a Minister, as, for instance, when compulsorily acquiring land. In certain cases the consent of the Minister is needed for a local authority to sell or exchange land, appropriate land for a purpose other than that for which it was acquired, and purchase land not immediately required for a statutory purpose.[1] Many Acts require a Minister to adjudicate in a dispute between a local authority and an individual, although in some cases this type of dispute may be settled in a court of law.[4]

Central—local Communications

The extensive administrative control by central government of local authority activities necessitates regular communications between them, much of which takes place through correspondence. Another form of contact is through circulars, which can have any of the following functions.

1. Explanatory – drawing attention to and explaining the background, philosophy and objectives of new legislation affecting local authorities.
2. Directory – requiring local authorities to take specific action. This may be a statutory power when the circular becomes an instrument of delegated legislation. Alternatively, the circular may advise on administrative procedures, such as the method of submitting housing proposals to the Minister for approval.
3. Recommendatory – when a Minister recommends that local authorities shall take certain action in cases where they have discretion. For example, Ministers have urged local authorities to introduce differential rent schemes even though they had no statutory power to do so.
4. Advisory – offering advice and guidance, as, for instance, on how to deal with a particular type of planning application.
5. Seeking information on certain local government functions.

The Local Government Act 1972 was followed by the issue of

numerous circulars giving information on the implementation of local government reorganisation.

Another method of communication is by personal contact. Hence senior local government officers frequently visit Government departments for informal discussions with senior civil servants on local authority proposals. In this way the likely Ministry reaction can be determined and taken into consideration before too much detailed work is carried out on the proposed schemes. Where local authorities encounter serious problems they may send a small deputation of members and officers to London to discuss the matter with civil servants or possibly even a Minister. Stevenson[6] has described how local government officers have been known to form an alliance with their opposite numbers in Whitehall to ensure that their authority receives consistent advice or is subjected to consistent pressure.

Financial Control

Government departments generally have limited concern over the amount which a local authority may spend out of rate income. There are however a few cases where the law imposes a limit on the rate which can be levied for a particular purpose, such as the provision of entertainments, but these instances are few.[1]

Financial control does however constitute the most effective form of central government control of local authorities and it is effected through loans, grants and audit. By a skilful exercise of financial powers a Minister can compel a proper performance of duties and require local authorities to submit to inspections, make returns, provide information and even conform to departmental policy.[2]

Loans

Substantial central control becomes operative whenever local authorities require loans, as ministerial consent is usually necessary before they can borrow money. As shown in Chapter 7, local authorities generally require loans to finance large capital projects such as schools, housing and major highway schemes. The Minister can by the inclusion of conditions in the loan-sanction affect a local authority's policy. Furthermore, the Minister will need to satisfy himself that the purpose of the loan is desirable and that the amount is reasonable. However, refusal of loan-sanction does not preclude the local authority from financing the project out of rate income.[1]

Statutory borrowing powers almost invariably require the consent of the Minister. Even when borrowing powers are derived from local

Acts, the Ministers becomes involved in one way or another. Control over the borrowing of local authorities should rest in one department to help ensure the financial stability of authorities. For this reason, the consent of the Minister is required, for example, for educational loans, although he will consult with the appropriate Government department.[2]

By central control over loan-sanctions the Government can ensure that capital expenditure by local authorities conforms to the national economic programme. Furthermore, the Treasury has considerable influence on the rate of interest at which money can be borrowed, and when this is raised, the cost of local authority capital projects is also increased and this may result in a reduction in the number of schemes being implemented.

Grants

As shown in Chapter 7, the income of local government in England and Wales from central government grants far exceeds the revenue from rates, and so local authorities are very much dependent upon central government support from this source. The various forms of Exchequer grant were considered in Chapter 7 and it will have been noted that they can be classified under two heads: specific grants in aid of particular services; and general or block grants.

Specific grants provide central government with the greatest opportunity to exercise quite detailed control of local authority activities, as a grant will not generally be payable unless the appropriate Minister is reasonably satisfied with the service for which the grant is claimed, and in most cases grant-earning expenditure must be 'approved expenditure'. Although grants are rarely withheld, the possibility enables Government departments on occasions to influence considerably the form of local authority services.[3] The power to withhold or reduce grants is a subtle and effective form of central control, as most local authorities are anxious to obtain grants, especially in connection with expensive services, even at the price of submitting themselves to supervision and possibly direction in some cases. Departmental approval, carrying with it the promise of grant, is essential for the implementation of most major capital projects. This form of central control also ensures that these particular local authority activities accord with national policy and interests.[2] Typical examples of specific grants are police grants and housing subsidies.

The most important general grant is the rate support grant, which consists of a global sum determined by the Minister and approved by the House of Commons, and which is distributed to local authorities on the basis of a complex population-weighted formula.

It constitutes a block grant which may be spent by local authorities on any of their services without the need for prior central government approval. However, any Minister involved with a service provided by a local authority can take steps to reduce the amount of the rate support grant where a local authority fails to achieve a reasonable standard, quite apart from the right to reduce the rate of grant generally. Nevertheless, the Minister must give the local authority the opportunity to make representations and he has to secure the approval of the House of Commons to the proposed reduction.[5] The rate support grant is a wide embracing provision and enables central government to influence the whole range of local authority activities.

The main advantage to central government of the grants system is that, in times of economic crisis, the Government can restrict local authority spending, merely by altering the level of grants. This in its turn causes resentment among local authorities which regard the extent of the central control as excessive.

District Audit

Nature and Form of Audit

District audit is concerned with checking local authority accounts to ensure that the expenditure is proper and legal. The extent to which it is or can be an instrument of central control is questionable. The auditor's functions are judicial in character, since he inquires, amongst other things, into the legality of a local authority's expenditure. He is, moreover, independent of the Minister and is not answerable to him, and the Minister cannot be questioned in Parliament as to the auditor's decisions. Challenging of the auditor's decisions is by way of appeal to the High Court. Nevertheless, the district audit is historically one of the more important ways in which Parliament secures the subordination of local authorities to its will as prescribed by statute,[3] and stems from the most unsatisfactory way in which the poor law was administered in some areas, which has been aptly described by Thornhill.[7]

With the exception of London, the Local Government Act 1972 permits local authorities to choose between district and professional audit, but an appointment of a professional auditor must be approved by the Minister. Richards[4] found that only three counties and seven metropolitan districts use professional audit and half of these retain district audit to check some of their accounts. Professional audit can lead to lengthy delays when the professional auditor submits a critical report.

Appointment and Duties of Auditors

The Local Government Act 1972 requires every local authority to have its accounts audited, either by a district auditor or an approved auditor (a professionally qualified auditor approved by the Minister). District auditors are civil servants and are assigned by the Minister to certain districts, but local authorities contribute towards their salaries. Although civil servants, district auditors are, as has been shown, independent of the Minister.

The district auditor's duties go beyond the checking of accounts with vouchers. He must satisfy himself that the accounts have been prepared in proper form, satisfy legal requirements and have been prepared in accordance with good accounting practice. Apart from these technical matters he must consider whether the public interest requires him to report on any matters arising out of the accounts, so that they can be considered by the authority or brought to the attention of the public.[2]

District Audit Procedure

The accounts for the financial year ending 31 March must be deposited at the offices of the local authority at least seven days before the audit commences, and during that period interested persons may inspect the documents and take extracts from them. Notice of the audit must be published in local newspapers, and at the commencement of the audit any local government elector may appear before the district auditor and raise objections to any item in the accounts.

A district auditor who considers an item of account contrary to law may apply to the court for a declaration to this effect, unless the expenditure has been sanctioned by the Minister. Where the court makes the declaration, it may order repayment by the person concerned and rectification of the accounts. Where the person concerned is a member of the local authority and the expenditure exceeds £2000, he may be disqualified for a specified period. The court, in making the order, must have regard to the person's ability to pay. Furthermore, it cannot make an order if satisfied that the person acted reasonably or in the belief that the expenditure was authorised by law.

Where a person has failed to bring into account a sum which ought to have been included, and where there is loss or deficiency due to wilful misconduct, the district auditor may certify a sum recoverable by the local authority from the person responsible. If that person is a member of the local authority and the amount exceeds £2000, he may be disqualified from membership for a period of five years.

The appropriate court is normally the High Court, but where the sum involved does not exceed the amount over which county courts have jurisdiction in actions on contract, the county court has concurrent jurisdiction with the High Court.

Auditors have right of access to documents which they consider necessary for audit purposes, and failure to produce is a criminal offence. An approved auditor is liable to penalties if he wrongfully discloses information which is made available to him in the course of audit. An approved auditor cannot impose sanctions; he reports to the Minister, who may direct the holding of an extraordinary audit by the district auditor. The Minister has wide powers for making regulations relating to the keeping of accounts and audit procedures.

A good example of the type of action taken by a district auditor, albeit under pre-1972 powers, with the subsequent appeal is now described. In *Taylor* v. *Munrow* (1960), St Pancras Metropolitan Borough Council had a duty to charge tenants of requisitioned housing the full economic rent based on the compensation rent payable to the owners, with power to reduce the amount if a tenant was unable to meet the full rent. The Council declined to operate a means test and reduced the rents of all the tenants. The loss incurred and charged to the rates was disallowed and surcharged by the district auditor, whose decision was confirmed on appeal to the court.[5]

Advantages of District Audit

The main objection to district audit has been that it empowers a government official – albeit an independent one acting quasi-judicially – to impose penalties on elected representatives for using their judgement on how best to serve their electors. Further that surcharges were not merely on illegal expenditure but also on expenditure considered to be unreasonable. The Local Government Act 1972 simplified the arrangements and the district auditor is now concerned only with legality. Additionally, he no longer imposes penalties for presumed illegality, but requests a court to do so. The amount of criticism of the district audit system has declined as local authorities have become increasingly accustomed to a wide range of central government administrative controls, and are now much less likely to engage in excessive or improper spending.[4]

Thornhill[7] believes that the district audit system represents one of the surest ways of maintaining the financial integrity of local authorities by providing them with independent testimony to the state of their financial health. The district auditor also plays his part along with local officers in securing and maintaining high standards of accounting and financial control. At annual audits the district auditor collaborates with and takes full account of the work of internal audit staffs. In addition many local authorities, particularly the smaller ones, turn to the auditor for advice on unusual or complicated problems.

Appeals, Default Powers and Settlement of Disputes

Appeals

Where a local authority is given a power to act in a way which may interfere with private property or adversely affect another public body, it is customary to make statutory provision for appeals against the actions of the local authority. In some cases the appeals will be heard by the courts and in other cases by the appropriate Minister. For example, an applicant for planning permission who is aggrieved by the decision of the planning authority can appeal to the Minister under the Town and Country Planning Act 1971. Likewise where a local authority seeks to acquire land by compulsory purchase, persons affected have the right to make objections to the Minister. Another statute containing a similar right of appeal is the Highways Act 1959, in this case against certain decisions of local authorities acting under the street works codes. All these provisions tend to reduce the powers of local authorities by making them subservient to the Minister and yet, at the same time, help in safeguarding the interests of the private individual against the State.

Default Powers

Acts of Parliament which impose duties upon local authorities usually also contain a provision that if the local authority fails to perform its duty, the appropriate Minister may after due inquiry declare the authority to be in default. The steps to be taken by the Minister vary according to the provisions of the relevant statute. In some cases a Minister may himself perform the local authority's function.[1] Default powers aim at preventing the breakdown of essential services through the failure of local authorities to perform their duties.

Where a local authority has defaulted in the discharge of certain functions, including library and welfare services, the appropriate Minister may transfer the functions to himself. Another course of action is for the Minister to issue a formal order directing the defaulting authority to take necessary action within a prescribed period. Non-compliance with the order will result in the issue of an order of court (mandamus) against the authority, and subsequent failure to act could result in the arrest or fining of members or officers of the authority.[1]

Yet a further course of action is for the Minister to transfer the powers of a defaulting authority to another authority. For example, where a county district council defaults in its public health or housing duties, the Minister may transfer these functions to the county council. Under the Housing Finance Act 1972 the Minister may make a default order and subsequently appoint a housing commissioner to discharge prescribed housing duties in the name of the local authority, working through and with the assistance of the authority's own staff, together with such staff of his own as he may appoint. This provision was implemented at Clay Cross in 1973–4, when the Labour council refused to operate the Conservative Housing Finance Act.

The Education Act 1944 confers wide default powers on the Secretary of State for Education and Science where local education authorities, or managers or governors of any county or voluntary school, fail to discharge any statutory duty. The Secretary of State is empowered to make an order declaring the authority, or the managers or governors, to be in default, and giving such directions as appear expedient. These directions are enforceable in the courts.

Default powers are seldom implemented but their existence provides the means of ensuring the performance of statutory duties relating to local authority services. Some believe that the mere existence of default powers and the threat implied in their existence are sufficient to induce local authorities to perform their duties effectively. Others argue with considerable justification that the excellent record of the majority of local authorities stems from the pressure of public opinion and the desire of most authority members to give good service.[1]

Settlement of Disputes

Many statutes provide for disputes between local authorities to be referred to the appropriate Minister for settlement. For example, a dispute as to the financial responsibility for a pupil is referred to the Secretary of State for Education and Science. In like manner many statutes provide for disputes between local authorities and their officers to be referred to a Minister. For example, dismissed police constables can appeal to the Home Secretary and superannuation disputes can be referred to the Secretary of State for the Environment.

Control through Inspection

Inspection of Services

Inspection by central government officers formed an early and important component of the central control mechanism of local government. Power is conferred by various statutes to undertake the supervision of local authority services by means of inspectors. This system has two main objectives.

1. To examine and assist in maintaining the efficiency of the particular service.
2. To provide a link between Government departments and those concerned with the administration of the service, to promote the exchange of ideas and to facilitate the pooling of the experience of different authorities.

Practical examples of this fairly restricted form of control follow.

The Education Act 1944 places a duty on the Secretary of State for Education and Science to cause an inspection to be made of every educational establishment at such intervals as he considers appropriate and to arrange a special inspection of any establishment whenever he thinks it desirable.

The Police Act 1964 provides for the appointment of inspectors of constabulary who have a duty to inspect and to report to the Home Secretary on the efficiency of police forces, and to carry out such other duties for furthering police efficiency as the Home Secretary may direct.

The Fire Service Act 1947 enables the Crown and the Secretary of State to appoint inspectors who are to obtain information on how fire authorities carry out their functions and on technical matters relating to the fire service.

Inspectorate and Inquiries

Under various statutes Government departments are required or authorised to hold local inquiries on a variety of occasions. The Local Government Act 1972 prescribes the general arrangements and duties of inspectors. Inspectors are central government officers who when conducting an inquiry may, within prescribed limits, require any person to attend and give evidence on oath or produce documents, and the costs may be charged to such local authority or party to the inquiry as the inspector may direct. Another but simpler form of local inquiry is the informal hearing before a person who is appointed by the Minister and who does not possess the special powers of an inspector holding a local inquiry, such as the power to hear evidence on oath.[2]

Where a local authority makes a clearance order to acquire compulsorily an area of sub-standard housing, and owners of property appeal, the Ministry will arrange for an inspector to hold a local inquiry and to hear objections and claims. Local inquiries may also be held to consider appeals against planning refusals and to hear objections to compulsory purchase orders of local authorities. An inspector does not usually make a decision but listens to the evidence submitted by both parties, visits the site and makes a report and recommendation to the Minister. The Minister makes the final decision in the light of the inspector's report, which is normally made public.[4]

Approval of Schemes

Many statutes impose on local authorities a duty to prepare 'schemes' or 'proposals' or 'plans' setting out how they propose to carry out their statutory duties, for approval by the appropriate Minister. The statute provides the broad framework and each authority is required to work out in some detail how the Act will be administered in its area, the nature and extent of the services proposed and the lines of future development, thus ensuring reasonable flexibility in operation to meet local needs. After approval the scheme is binding upon the authority, and provision is made for amendments adopting similar procedures.

Several examples of this form of control follow.

The Town and Country Planning Act 1968 requires each planning authority to survey its area and prepare a structure plan for submission to the Minister. A structure plan consists of a written statement supplemented by diagrams and illustrations showing the authority's policy and general proposals for development in its area. A planning authority may also prepare a local plan for any part of its area showing the authority's proposals for the development and other use of the land, and indicating the measures the authority thinks fit for the improvement of the physical environment and management of traffic. The Education Act 1944 requires local education authorities to prepare development plans for the provision of sufficient primary and secondary schools in their areas. Local authorities were also required to submit long-term development plans for the social services in 1972.

Through the approval of schemes, plans and proposals, government departments are able to exert considerable influence on the way in which local authority services are planned and administered. This procedure ensures that each local authority's proposals are of adequate standard without being excessively extravagant, and that together they attain some measure of uniformity throughout the country. Government departments often prepare model schemes as guidelines for local authorities, and it is customary for discussions to be held between central and local officers at the formative stage of development plans.[3]

Effect of Central Control

By the various measures described in this chapter, central government can influence significantly local authority actions. Apart from investigating notified matters, Ministers and their officers may inquire into and inspect the work of local authorities and may retard their activities by refusing sanction or approval, by withholding a grant, or by over-ruling a local authority on appeal. Should an authority fail to perform its duty, default powers can be used. By regulations, local authorities are given direction as to their activities.[1]

Although collectively these measures appear to result in a formidable degree of supervision of local authorities by central government, authorities have a considerable degree of freedom and scope for alternative action, subject to the availability of adequate finance. Central government is concerned to see that local government operates effectively and would not wish to interfere to such an extent as to jeopardise this. Local authorities are given plenty of opportunity to formulate and, after approval, to implement proposals aimed at meeting local needs. In general the Minister only intervenes to ensure that an authority is doing its work properly and Parliament must, of necessity, require adequate safeguards when so much public money is involved.

The Layfield Committee[8] in 1976 expressed fears that local government was becoming overdominated by central government, and considered that some central controls were now being used for purposes for which they were not originally intended. The Maud Report[9] criticised the detailed central government supervision and believed in 1967 that this could be relaxed with stronger and fewer local authorities.

In practice the legal powers of control vested in Ministers and Government departments are generally exercised with tact and understanding. Consultation takes place continuously between central and local government and local authorities are never backward in pressing their claims. On wider issues Ministers and their departments consult with local authority associations so that a reasonable level of understanding is achieved.

References

1. JACKSON, W. E., *The Structure of Local Government in England and Wales* (Longman, 1966).

2. HART, W. O. and GARNER, J. F., *Hart's Introduction to the Law of Local Government and Administration* (Butterworth, 1973).
3. CROSS, C. A., *Principles of Local Government Law* (Sweet and Maxwell, 1974).
4. RICHARDS, P. G., *The Reformed Local Government System* (Allen and Unwin, 1975).
5. CLARKE, H. W., *Administrative Law for Surveying Students* (Sweet and Maxwell, 1970).
6. STEVENSON, B., 'Local and central government relationships', *Public Finance and Accountancy*, October 1976.
7. THORNHILL, W., *The Growth and Reform of English Local Government* (Weidenfeld and Nicolson, 1971).
8. Cmnd. 6453, *Report of the Committee of Enquiry on Local Government Finance* – the Layfield Committee (H.M.S.O., 1976).
9. *Report of the Committee on the Management of Local Government* – the Maud Report (H.M.S.O., 1967).

CHAPTER TEN

LOCAL GOVERNMENT NEEDS AND THE FUTURE

Public Relations

Communication

The larger size of local authorities and the greater complexity of their arrangements and activities in recent years tends to cause the electorate to lose interest in community matters and can, ultimately, result in the individual abrogating his responsibilities to society. Richards[1] has described how local government is nevertheless the smallest and most approachable unit in our system of public administration and should accordingly be able to play a major role in breaking down barriers between the individual and society. It is easier to influence local decisions than national ones. Yet there is widespread indifference as shown by the low polls at local government elections and the research undertaken by the Government Social Survey for the Maud Committee.[2] In this survey over one-quarter of those interviewed were unable to name any service provided by their borough or district council, increasing to nearly one-half for county councils.

The Bains Report[3] considered at some length public relations aspects in the post-1974 county and district councils. The Study Group believed that local government reorganisation in 1974 would bring into sharp focus the deficiencies of public relations within many local authorities. In the Group's view the public have a right to information about the affairs of their local council and the Group believed that access to council and committee meetings could well stimulate the public's desire to be better informed. In evidence to the Group, the Institute of Public Relations Local Government Group gave a list of functions performed by public relations units in local government, and these included press relations, provision of various information services, liaison with various local organisations, preparation of certain publications, reports and leaflets, and publicity and organisation of civic events. The Study Group recommended that authorities should publish an annual report showing the past allocation of resources and identifying the major problems facing them, and their plans for solving them.

It is important that a local authority should take every opportunity to explain its policies and the underlying reasons to the electorate, and that it should be receptive to fair comment. Fortunately the importance of good public relations is being increasingly recognised in local government. Nevertheless there are still some councils which shroud their meetings in secrecy, consider their actions sacrosanct and resist any form of public involvement. Local government exists to serve the local community and, as far as practicable, meet its needs. It should be seen to be endeavouring to achieve these objectives.

Local Press

As outlined in Chapter 6, the Public Bodies (Admission to Meetings) Act 1960 gives the public the right to attend council meetings, meetings of an education committee with delegated powers or of any committee consisting of all of the members of the council. The public, including the press, may however be excluded by resolution where publicity would be prejudicial to the public interest by reason of the confidential nature of the business or for other special reasons contained in the resolution and arising from the nature of the business. Such a special reason might, for instance, be the need to consider advice from officers. There are also specific provisions in the Act covering notice of an open meeting and the supply of agenda to the press where requested. The Local Government Act 1972 applied the provisions of the 1960 Act to committees, joint committees and advisory committees appointed by local authorities.

Hence a local authority can no longer exclude the press merely by resolving themselves into a council in committee, and the precise grounds for exclusion on a particular item of business must be stated. In too many cases the local press is treated as a potential enemy of the council rather than as an aid in informing public opinion. Councils often seem to be afraid of press misrepresentation or of adverse press criticism and some councils dislike their proceedings being made public. In the interests of democratic local government, the press should be given every assistance and encouragement to report on all council proceedings, except for certain special matters like the placing of contracts and confidential staffing items, and to offer such informed comments as considered appropriate. The *Nottingham Evening Post* survey of local government salaries in Nottinghamshire before and after reorganisation in 1974,[4] although heavily criticised at the time, rendered good public service by drawing attention to the escalating cost of provision of local authority services.

Some criticism can however be levelled at the press, as even when full facilities are provided, a considerable number of local newspapers report council proceedings in a haphazard and inadequate way. All too frequently the only local government business which reaches the front page is an argument between councillors, possibly concerned with a mere triviality, or some other matter of so-called 'human interest', while the more important and fundamental issues confronting the council receive minimal attention. In general the standard of reporting and criticism of local government affairs is disappointingly low. It is difficult to establish whether this stems from lack of interest by or education of journalists, or lack of interest among the papers' readers. Both factors are present, especially the latter, as it should be borne in mind that newspapers generally try to give readers what they want. On the other hand some local newspapers report and comment in a comprehensive and masterly way for the benefit of the public.

The Maud Committee[2] recommended that local authorities should regard the press as partners in the process of informing and educating the public. Local authorities are requested to appreciate the difficulties which face the press, such as limitations of time and the variable calibre of reporters, and to enter into mutually convenient arrangements for the handling of material. To assist the press in this work, local authorities are advised to provide adequate facilities, such as press rooms and access to and free use of telephones.

Unfortunately not all local authorities are complying with the statutory requirements aimed at keeping the electorate better informed. The proviso allowing for exclusions in circumstances prejudicial to the public interest is sometimes used in a way that the legislators could never have intended. In 1974 one councillor of a district council withdrew from a meeting of the council in protest when the press was excluded so that a discussion of staff loans totalling more than £40 000 could be held in 'secret'. At the same time a county council resolved that the press should not be admitted to meetings of sub-committees. These decisions run contrary to the generally accepted theme – 'open government is good government'.

Burke[5] believes that a firmly worded departmental circular is needed requesting local authorities to adhere to the spirit of the law. Better understanding between local authorities and journalists could be achieved by representatives of local authority associations consulting with press representatives on a continuing basis. Burke has suggested the setting up of a joint committee or even a permanent standing committee to deal with current problems and, ideally, to produce a joint memorandum giving guidance to all local authorities, public relations officers, councillors with particular interests in relations with the press, and to local editors and their local government reporters. Improved understanding could be generated by local authorities inviting editors and their reporters on regular tours of departments so that they are familiar with the institutional background.

A local editor can also assist by preparing a manual on local authority reporting for use by his staff. The manual could usefully contain a breakdown of the administrative functions of the local authority, detailing the responsibilities of each department, the names and locations of the senior officers in each department and particulars of the councillors serving on each committee. Appendices might contain such information as notes on the law relating to members' interests and admission of the press and public to meetings. If the manual is prepared in a loose-leaf format it can be readily updated and the reporter can insert useful local information that he acquires on the job.[5]

Public Relations Officers

During the 1960s various local authorities appointed public relations officers to explain their policies to the public. This need increased with the creation of larger local authorities in 1974. Such officers have a valuable role to play but this must not be taken as a reason for elected members to reduce their informative activities. For example, it is much more satisfactory for the chairman of the housing committee to explain the council's housing policy to the press, rather than the public relations officer.

The public relations officer also interprets the wishes of the electorate and conveys them to the council, and this provides an additional and authorised channel for complaints and suggestions. At the same time the complexity and scope of modern local government activities creates the need for a full-time qualified officer to operate the information service.

Local authorities can only hope to forge a satisfactory and effective partnership between the electorate, elected members and local authority officers for the benefit of the community when each has full knowledge and understanding of the needs, aspirations and difficulties of the others. A positive, energetic and sympathetic approach is needed to foster and promote such a partnership. Ideally public relations staff should have a journalistic background, which will help in deciding how and where to place material to optimum advantage. Full use should be made of local radio and television stations as valuable communication links, particularly for publicising achievements and explaining policies. On occasions popular local programmes can incorporate local government matters. Additionally the issuing of press statements and the holding of press conferences on important issues can be beneficial.

The Bains Study Group[3] urged the larger local authorities to establish a public relations and information unit. The Study Group also recommended local authorities to produce an annual report containing details of the authority's services and plans to solve present problems, to assist in promoting public understanding of local government. Attractive house styles incorporating a distinguishing symbol in advertisements and on local authority communications assist in enhancing the authority's public image.[6] Posters, exhibitions, public meetings and leaflets can all be used in imaginative ways to keep the public informed of local authority activities.

The Greater London Council has established an extensive research library to assist in discharging its duty under the London Government Act to 'collect and make information available about Greater London'. The library provides a recognised point of contact for officers, members, the London boroughs, Members of Parliament and the public. The range of computerised information provided is very wide, including technical information, general background information, political data, internal unpublished information and constituency data. An on-going index to council minutes enables members to trace more easily and quickly documents, questions and the like.[7]

It is the experience of the Greater London Council that the provision of an objective information service which is neither committed to existing policy nor politically biased has an important part to play in local government. Hender[8] emphasised this aspect when he wrote 'there does appear to be a quaint notion in local government that the mere fact of receiving the majority of votes at the ballot box automatically qualifies a person to play a full role in the policy-making of his authority and makes him capable of dealing with a myriad of complaints, suggestions and problems from his constituency with virtually no assistance from official sources other than the receipt of an agenda and supporting documents – usually less than a week before he has to make an important decision'.

The National and Local Government Officers' Association (NALGO) in its evidence to the Maud Committee[2] very aptly and succinctly described the public relations function in the following terms: 'In the one direction it must use every available medium of communication to explain the local authority to the public, ensuring that its aspirations, and policies, the services it provides, its methods of working, its achievements and plans, and its difficulties and problems, are understood and that the public is encouraged to co-operate with it. In the other direction it must seek to explain the public to the local authority, keeping a finger on the pulse of popular need and opinion, and surveying, analysing and conveying the results of its inquiries to those responsible for the direction of policy, nationally and locally.'

Commissioners for Local Administration

The machinery for the submission, consideration and deciding of citizens' grievances against a local authority is described in Chapter 8. The increasing powers of both central and local government to make decisions affecting various rights of the citizen make it necessary to provide effective remedies which protect him against unjust administrative action.

The establishment of Commissioners for Local Administration can be justified on the following grounds.

1. Councillors, however anxious they are to look after citizens' interests, are not well suited to carry out independent investigations of this kind.
2. Senior local government officers, however competent, are unlikely to be regarded as independent.
3. A local commissioner can restore public confidence in a local authority, by showing that the complaints are ill-founded.
4. The larger authorities created in 1974 are more remote from the public than their predecessors.

Holdsworth,[9] while recognising that the Commission provides a valuable safety valve for the individual who feels increasingly caught up in the magnitude or bureaucracy of the public services, feels that 'maladministration' is an unfortunate term to apply to many of the complaints received by the Ombudsman. Some of the complaints investigated have revealed serious injustice and real culpability; others show little more than a failure to achieve administrative perfection but can still result in considerable adverse publicity. On the debit side the possible dangers are that the system could unfortunately result in actions and decisions being transferred up the hierarchy, local authorities doing only the statutory minimum, a reduction of informal and flexible working arrangements and the introduction of wasteful and counterproductive changes in working methods.

Co-operation between Authorities

Various reports on local government structure and management advocate maximum co-operation between local authorities in order to achieve maximum efficiency, best use of resources and avoidance of duplication. Some notable pre-1974 examples of joint local authority action include combined sports centres and expanding towns, both of which are now described.

Combined Sports Centres

Combined sports centres ensure better value for money and the provision of a wider range of facilities than would otherwise be obtainable. The Sports Council[10] has shown how it is possible to plan the entire physical education accommodation of a large new school for shared use with the community, the result being a sports complex comprising pools, sports hall, gymnasia, squash courts, playing facilities and social provision. The school use and community use are complementary, as schools mostly want facilities during weekdays, and the public in the evenings, at weekends and on holidays.[11]

Excellent examples of this type of joint provision are the combined sports centres provided alongside new comprehensive schools by Nottinghamshire County Council in collaboration with various district councils. The county council offered a site, car parking space and architectural and quantity surveying services free of charge, while reduced prices flow from the larger contracts. In addition roads, sewers and landscaping form part of the building contract.[12] The first Nottinghamshire scheme was opened at Bingham in 1969 with the initial cost shared 35 per cent to the county council and 65 per cent to the district council. The county council as local education authority planned to receive 40 per cent of the use but agreed to meet 50 per cent of the net running costs.[13]

Expanding Towns

The Town Development Act 1952 enabled small country towns to be enlarged by their local authorities (receiving authorities) entering into agreements with large urban local authorities (exporting authorities). The Government provided a considerable measure of financial support and the county councils of the receiving areas often gave financial and technical assistance. The expanding towns usually received both population and industry from a large congested city to secure a well-balanced community in a static or declining town.

Typical of some fifty expansion agreements is the one entered into by the London County Council (now Greater London Council) and Haverhill Urban District Council (now part of St Edmundsbury District Council) in 1957. The author[14] has described how the initial scheme provided for the erection of about 1500 dwellings in addition to shops, schools and ancillary buildings, for the provision of open spaces and for the development of industrial sites. The former London County Council agreed to carry out the housing and ancillary development and the provision of roads and sewers on industrial sites, as well as initially financing land acquisition and housing and industrial development until it became revenue-earning, and giving financial assistance in other ways. These were generous terms and enabled the small receiving authority satis-factorily to bridge a difficult interim period when contractors were receiving large monthly payments for constructional work long before receipt of any income from completed dwellings or factories. In addition the former West Suffolk County Council contributed to the extensions of sewers and sewage treatment works, and the Government also contributed towards the cost of services and paid housing subsidies.

Many of the expansion schemes are now being terminated because of the reduction in the forecasts of total population and of the depopulation of inner cities. Although the extent of the redistribution of population and industry nationally achieved by the expanding towns is relatively small, nevertheless these towns have acquired a new prosperity and vitality and provided good working and living conditions for many families. The schemes have also shown a new level of co-operation between local authorities – so different from the mutual distrust which had occurred so frequently in the past.

Shared and Inter-related Functions

The Local Government Act 1972 split a number of functions between county councils and district councils, and this was accompanied by the establishment of water and health authorities. These develop-ments created a need for inter-authority decision-making founded on a high level of co-operation and understanding. The shared planning function is a notable example, with strategic planning performed at county level and local planning and development control at district level. Strategic planning however has implications for other district functions such as housing and leisure services. Hence strategic decisions taken by one authority have considerable influence on tactical decisions made by another. Satisfactory operation requires good communication between the participating authorities and full appreciation of common issues.[15]

Many local authorities set up working groups at both officer and member level where areas of decision-making overlap. These formal arrangements are usually supported by a network of informal relationships between the authorities. Overlapping membership of county and district councils and local authority representation has assisted.

The Sunderland Study[16] attempts to show how inter-authority collaboration between counties and districts can operate. It involves formulating a 'collaboration plan' setting out the functions and responsibilities between the two tiers, highlighting critical activities requiring joint or co-ordinated action, matching the organisation to the tasks, aligning management processes and planning cycles, and co-ordinating data resources. Collaborative plans can usefully be employed for development plan schemes and in the implementation of agency arrangements for such services as leisure, highways and refuse disposal. These arrangements lead to efficient provision of services and avoid wasteful duplication.

Community plans can be prepared to embrace the whole range of local government services. They can provide a common appreciation of matters such as urban deprivation and how they should be handled by the two tiers. The housing action area approach provides an opportunity to co-ordinate district housing and public health functions with the social services of county councils. Furthermore, some county councils are establishing sophisticated computer facilities to provide county-wide information services for district councils.[15]

Blessley[17] has described how the former London County Council provided extensive housing estates and established massive land banks prior to 1963. The London Government Act 1963 made the boroughs the prime agencies for housing in London but the Greater London Council was given concurrent powers which continue to operate with the consent of the Minister.

The London borough councils faced problems in expanding their housing activities to such a significant extent, but in 1970 a total of 50 000 dwellings were transferred to the boroughs leaving about 210 000 in G.L.C. management, although this figure increases at the rate of 4000 to 5000 per annum. Some of the boroughs are pressing for further transfers but wish to be selective, having regard to the age, condition and outstanding debt of the property. Co-operation in this instance is not particularly satisfactory and there is a need for a single strategic housing authority for Greater London to operate centralised control.

Neighbourhood Councils and Other Voluntary Groups

Pressure or Voluntary Groups

In recent years the number of groups of people formed to bring pressure to bear on local authorities has increased considerably. These groups generally cut across party lines and enable views to be aired which might not be possible through normal party channels. Their main value is not so much in what they achieve but that through their activities they secure public discussion of important local matters. For example, residents' associations and amenity associations forge valuable links between electors and local authorities, providing a useful two-way exchange of information. Local authorities and their elected members need to be cognisant of grass roots problems, needs and views.

Neighbourhood Councils

The Redcliffe-Maud Report[18] was widely criticised for favouring efficiency over local democracy by recommending the withdrawal of existing functions from parish councils and making them merely advisory bodies. Subsequently the Department of the Environment circulated a consultative paper in 1975[19] proposing a statutory scheme to give neighbourhood councils a legal status and thereby increase the standing of rural parishes. The paper outlined the aims of neighbourhood councils as stimulating self-help, providing special facilities, representing local desires and preferences to government and firms, and fostering a sense of local responsibility, particularly among the young.

Jackson[20] has described how 22 neighbourhood or community councils had been established in Stockport by 1977, each with an elected representative membership of local people advised by a community development officer, meeting monthly. The matters discussed range widely from redevelopment, slum clearance, compulsory purchase orders and general improvement areas to housing, highways, refuse collection, recreation, social, education and planning matters. The principal method of operation is to correspond with the district council describing the problem and asking what action it would take. Minutes of the neighbourhood/ community council meetings form an item on the agenda of the district council's area committees, and there is an interchange of members at both bodies' meetings. The district council gives each neighbourhood/community council an annual grant to cover running costs.

Hence the neighbourhood/community council acts as a local collection point for problems for transmission to the district council, and this results in the local authority being less remote from the people it serves by responding to locally perceived needs. However, at a time when local authority services and capital expenditure programmes are being reduced, it becomes progressively more difficult for the local authority to respond to the neighbourhood/community council's requests and for the latter to maintain its impetus and to satisfy its members.[20]

Regionalism and Devolution

Since 1965 England has been divided into eight regions for the purpose of economic planning, and in 1974 regional water authorities and regional health authorities were created. The Royal Commission on the Constitution[21] envisaged the setting up of regional institutions in England in parallel with devolution to elected assemblies in Scotland and Wales. Local authorities generally fear that developments of this kind are likely to diminish their status and powers, and provide a barrier between them and central government.[1] Another approach is not to provide a further tier but to replace county councils by regional authorities with extended functions and to strengthen the district councils. It can be argued with some justification that the current areas of local authorities have not been delineated with much thought for their functions, whether in operating services or representing local inhabitants, but by reference to political, historical and other considerations.[22]

A Government discussion paper in 1974[23] outlined the various ways in which devolution might take place within the United Kingdom. Some proposals incorporate power solutions, with a significant degree of power being devolved from central to semi-autonomous regional governments. Such forms of regional government might or might not have legislative powers. Other approaches incorporate information solutions, with the regional institutions being largely advisory or consultative in character, having little real power and with a main function of providing information aimed at influencing central and local government. One such approach would be to advise central government and co-ordinate local government activities. The power solutions generate more problems than the information ones, particularly in the area of finance. It is difficult to balance the need for national equality with the pressure for freedom and discretion at regional level.[24]

The Government declared in 1976 that it did not wish to change the local government structure should devolution take place. Himsworth[25] has however shown that, on devolution, local government itself will be a devolved subject with the assemblies overseeing the work of local authorities in devolved matters. In 1977 Parliament experienced difficulty in finding a system which would maintain the economic and fiscal integrity of the United Kingdom, while still permitting independent finance-raising powers for the Scottish Assembly.

The Impact of Reorganisation

The Changed Situation

Ashford[26] has described how political needs intervened in determining the pattern of local government reorganisation. Winning elections is an inevitable counterweight to the rational solution of the size and shape of local government units. The Conservatives were anxious to preserve the historic counties and to protect the wealthy suburbs and countryside from urban demands for housing space. Care was taken in delineating the boundary between Hampshire and Dorset in 1972 not to divide a safe Conservative seat, while the Conservative town of Newmarket might logically have been in Cambridgeshire but was retained in Suffolk to balance Labour strength. In general the new counties are not large enough nor are their boundaries appropriate for many of their functions. They do not relate well to the facts of social geography.

The Local Government Act 1972 introduced some fundamental changes in the structure of local government, including the demise of county boroughs and the inclusion of the larger urban areas into the government of counties. The payment of attendance allowances to councillors and the extension of service from three to four years are also significant. The merger of urban and rural areas has resulted in the extension of party politics in local government. Some officers have been faced with entirely different situations and approaches to those experienced before. The formation and development of pressure groups or voluntary organisations continues to grow, exerting further pressures on local authorities and their councillors. Many members of the public are now faced with more channels of communication through county and district councils, regional water authorities and area health authorities, and numerous advice centres, with a further possibility of statutory neighbourhood councils in urban areas.

There is more evidence of inter-authority conflict often resulting from shared functions. The metropolitan counties have endeavoured to define a clear role for themselves and have encountered resistance from their districts. On the political front strong party leadership has emerged accompanied by full-time politicians.[27]

On reorganisation, the number of seats on county councils reduced substantially, aldermen were abolished and many former members retired. The average age of councillors reduced and some authorities attracted more young executives and businessmen, but this was not universal.

Effect of Party Politics

It has been argued that the work of a local authority is routine, technical and uncontroversial, and to introduce party politics merely complicates the issues and the organisation of the authority. Rhodes[27] contends, with some justification, that 'politics is about conflicts over, and choices between, who gets what, when and how'. Local authorities in their allocation of resources cannot avoid such choices.

As outlined in Chapter 4 national and local issues can no longer be entirely divorced and the party system enables consistent policies to be pursued over reasonable periods of time, and ensures that councillors are made more responsive to the wishes of the electorate. Gyford[28] believes that strong and vigorous political parties can revitalise the elected member, whose impact he considers to be weakened by the increased technical expertise of officers and increasing public participation. Gyford is not opposed to clashes between parties in local government as he considers that this merely reflects the different opinions of parties and these represent different sectors of the community, but this view is unlikely to secure whole-hearted acceptance. He considers that the parties perform a valuable function in recruiting elected members and in bringing coherence to the work of the local authority, and advocates some full-time and salaried members supported by personal assistants and with adequate training and research facilities.

Party politics has a considerable influence on the way in which local authorities conduct their affairs, including the membership of committees. There is a noticeable tendency for the majority party to occupy all the posts of chairman and vice-chairman on committees and sub-committees. Group decisions made prior to committee meetings all too frequently bind party members and severely restrict the adoption of alternative policies and courses of action. The group control and strict party discipline imposed by the Labour Party has pressed the Conservatives, Liberals and Independents into more forceful tactics.

Mallaby[29] is opposed to increased party politics in local government and fears that people of experience and ability, attracted to local government by feelings of care and compassion for neighbouring communities, are turning away from service on district and county councils organised on a party political basis as they fail to see what party politics has to do with domestic issues. He considers that councillors will increasingly take instructions from the Conservative Central. Office or Transport House, and pay less attention to local aspirations and needs. These dangers are probably overdramatised but it is, nevertheless, incumbent upon all elected members representing political parties to fight against undue domination of their actions by central party policies.

Corporate Management

The nature and application of corporate management to local government was examined in Chapter 5. It aims at providing a wider framework within which departmental needs and actions can be related, thus providing a balancing mechanism. Stewart[30] identifies a danger in that management teams may see their role not as the setting of a framework, but the consideration of all the authorities' activities. He describes vividly how 'the processes of corporate management are drowning in seas of paper, policy and resources committees battle with endless agendas, management teams become another committee through which new proposals have to struggle, inter-disciplinary groups proliferate, and there is a danger that all activities are dealt with by corporate management. It has to be learnt that streets are not swept by inter-disciplinary groups '

Benington[31] believes that the most widespread public criticism of local government today concerns the failure of representation and accountability in the democratic process, rather than the problems of management. He found little evidence of local authorities using reorganisation as an opportunity to develop new structures to strengthen the role of the councillor as an 'elected representative' as opposed to a 'financial manager', or to test new opportunities for participative and accountable local government.

Officer/Member Relationships

Since 1974 there have been radical changes in local government stemming from the larger administrative areas, the corporate management approach, the changing role of the elected member and greater public involvement. Prior to reorganisation the local government service had in general become overprofessional, giving rise to the following dangers as identified by Kershaw[32] – remoteness of local authorities from the electorate, members' rubber stamping officers' decisions and policies, some committee chairmen being manipulated by chief officers, and local authorities becoming too departmentalised and fragmented.

Professional enthusiasm needs to be curbed on occasions and elected members with their familiarity of and sensitivity to public opinion are able to exert this steadying influence. One of the main functions of a member is to secure the best mix of professional advice in the context of community needs and available resources.

Effective local government thus requires an effective working partnership between officers and members.[32]

Sharpe[33] has described how this partnership is not easy to forge and preserve. Members are accountable to the electorate and are in a position of power, while officers have professional expertise and provide continuity. Changing political control means that officers must remain detached from the political scene to maintain integrity and, in some cases, to survive! To be effective a chief officer must, as described in Chapter 4, retain the credibility and respect of elected members.

Corruption

The nature and probable extent of corruption in local government was examined in Chapter 4. Prior to the Poulson affair it was widely accepted that Britain enjoyed a standard of conduct among those in public life which was second to none in the world. The Poulson multi-disciplinary architectural practice relied on bribery and fee-cutting to ensure an adequate workload to sustain the vast organisation, and the irregularities which came to light only through bankruptcy proceedings involved the investigation of some 300 people. This was followed by undesirable speculative land transactions and an 88-day trial which culminated in the conviction of a planning committee chairman on corruption and conspiracy charges.

The Salmon Commission[34] found that of the 179 people, excluding police officers, convicted of offences under the Prevention of Corruption Acts over the previous decade, there were 14 local authority members and 70 local government officers, which is very small indeed judged against total numbers.

Most of the serious crime in local government centred around planning decisions and development contracts. Many members enter public life with little preparation and find themselves handling financial matters on a very substantial scale. The power of decision-making which can lead to large gains can give rise to temptations. The Commission considered that the receipt of gifts and hospitality should be limited to a bare minimum and officers should be constantly reminded of the rules relating to conflicting interests. Special difficulties confront officers who know or suspect that leading members are guilty of corrupt practices, because of the personal risk involved; nevertheless, it is their duty to report their suspicions to senior officers or the police.[35] The Commission suggested that in corruption charges the burden of proof should rest on the defence and that, with the authority of a high court judge, the police should be allowed access to a suspect's financial records.

This matter must be kept in perspective and there is no doubt that the majority of councillors and officials are honest. There is however no room for complacency and constant vigilance is essential, with a special responsibility on leading members and senior officers to set for themselves and to enforce highest standards.[36] Blessley[17] believes that the relatively few serious cases of fraud or corruption are an outstanding testimony to the integrity of the vast majority of people who work in the British public services, and emphasises the stringent controls and safeguards which operate through open committees, the opposition, press, public in attendance, scrutiny panels, the Ombudsman and the district auditor.

Local Government Finance

The methods of financing local government and the ensuing problems were examined in some detail in Chapter 7. The financial problems of local authorities increased significantly in 1977–8, when the Government rate support grant was reduced from 65.5 to 61 per cent of local government expenditure, resulting in a reduction in working balances, increased rates, and cuts in local expenditure in real terms. In addition substantial cuts were made to capital programmes. For example, school building allocations were progressively reduced from £307 million in 1972–3 to £126 million in 1977–8, while a reduction over a few years in local authority house building programmes in south-east England from an annual average of £15 million to £2 million resulted in the disbanding of the South East Authorities Consortium in 1977.

The cuts in local authority expenditure resulted in a dramatic fall in recruitment and most vacancies are subject to close scrutiny before a decision is made as to whether or not to fill. Early retirements and natural wastage were common in 1976–7 and it is likely that these will continue for some years. Essex County Council forecast considerable redundancies in 1977 to keep rate increases to an acceptable level while many authorities experienced difficulties in maintaining staff establishments because of substantially reduced workloads. Many authorities rather unwisely built up large technical staffs based on the peak capital programmes of 1973, thus aggravating their problems. For example, West Norfolk District Council's capital budget dropped from £4.5 million in 1974 to £80 000 in 1977, mainly as a result of a decision to stop house building, cuts in rate support grant and the Greater London Council's withdrawal from the Kings Lynn town expansion scheme. Early warning notices of possible redundancies were served on all 390 white-collar staff.

The financing of local government needs reviewing, as highlighted in the Layfield Committee report[37] and described in Chapter 7. In particular the Committee recommended that rateable values should be based on capital values and that local authority finances should be supplemented by a local income tax. The first proposal was favoured by the Government in 1977 but the latter suggestion received little public support. The committee was also concerned about the control of local authority spending. It recognised that a system based on central accountability would 'almost certainly have to require the submission of local authority budgets for scrutiny and approval'.

Much of the increased local authority expenditure stems from outside pressures, and is aggravated by central government legislating for new expenditure and spending curbs at the same time. Costing of the implications of new legislation have not always been accurate, as for example the Health and Safety at Work measures introduced in 1974. There are still pressures for improved services, of which the principal examples are social services, housing, police, consumer protection, conservation, recreation, and support for arts and public transport, although it is becoming increasingly difficult to meet these demands with a standstill in resources.

The involvement of local government at the formative stage of Government White Paper proposals could result in a better understanding of their implications and better and more effective use of resources. Effective national planning requires a detailed knowledge of local government needs, requirements and problems. The present central/local government relationships restrict the power of local authorities to decide their limits of expenditure within quite narrow limits, and they urgently need some security of income at least for the period required to make major structural changes, say a minimum of two years.

Against a background of severe economic restraint, local authorities may have to review their programmes and to give increased emphasis to maintenance as against improvement of services. Some deferred programmes may need abandoning instead of postponing, and land banks accumulated during a period of expansion should be looked at afresh. The raising of productivity levels could achieve better value for money.[38] Hicks[39] goes further and suggests making the social services less open-ended and makes the controversial point that education costs could be reduced by raising the compulsory school age to six, and cutting but improving the intake to universities by raising A-level requirements. It would however be unwise to consider changes to any one part of the higher educational sector in isolation.

Central/Local Government Relationships

This important aspect was broadly examined in Chapter 9. There is considerable evidence that the democratic process is being eroded, along with local authorities' sense of responsibility, by the extent and nature of central government controls, the move towards uniformity and the unsympathetic statements made by government leaders. Although local authorities derive their powers from Parliament they do not exist solely for the benefit of Whitehall. They are responsible to the local electorate and they should formulate and implement policies designed to meet local needs.[40] Excessive distant control can be both disruptive and frustrating. In particular, local authorities should have much greater discretion in determining how their funds are spent.

The transfer of local services away from local government is particularly disturbing. The National Health Service Reorganisation Act 1973 took away the remaining personal health services of local authorities, while the Water Act 1973 left them with the minimal responsibilities of testing water purity and administering local sewerage needs. The Local Authority Social Services Act 1970 required local authorities to unify local social services under a single committee, with a director of social services whose appointment must be approved by the Minister, providing a consolidating and centralising impact.[26]

Stevenson[41] highlighted the vast number of statutory instruments being issued with an impact on local government, including on average two circulars a week from the Department of Health and Social Security. They cover a diverse and quite extraordinary range of subjects, and include notifying authorities that the best place to put an office used by members of the public is in a place where members of the public can find it, giving instructions on how to fit asbestos hoods to firemen's helmets, asking for forecasts of the probable proceeds of police land to be sold in 1981, and advising on the disposal of imported rodents at ports and airports. It is time that civil service direction of local government was restricted to macroeconomic management and the few areas impinging on local government which require major decisions at national level.

Major Problems Facing Local Government

Finance and Staffing

As indicated earlier in the chapter most local authorities face major problems stemming from public expenditure cuts and some over-provision of staff. The rates explosion which followed reorganisation stemmed mainly from the acquisition of new accommodation, engagement of new staff and policy developments for certain services.

At that time there seemed plenty of finance available and the public was requesting improved services. In a short space of three years the climate had reversed and retrenchment became the order of the day against a background of high inflation and unemployment.

Housing

Over the half-century up to 1972, local authorities had provided nearly six million dwellings and let them at low rents. The contribution to human happiness must have been enormous, particularly having regard to the changing central controls and policies to which the authorities have been subjected. Nevertheless, it has proved a very expensive service with the accumulated housing loan debt exceeding £12 000 million and with the annual Exchequer subsidy approaching £900 million in 1976. At the same time there were about one million unfit houses and probably a further two million lacking in one or more standard amenities. In addition there are the dwellings which, although not unfit by accepted standards, are unsatisfactory, such as flats in tower blocks and houses on unattractive housing estates lacking in social amenities. Although there is a crude surplus of dwellings over families, it would be very misleading to conclude that the housing shortage is more apparent than real.

The overall housing provision has been adversely affected by stringent and excessive rent control, which has drastically reduced the private rented sector. A carefully balanced solution is needed in between complete municipalisation and an unrestricted market mechanism. Some excellent advice has been given by the Royal Institution of Chartered Surveyors,[42] which recommended that local authority housing should be restricted to areas of proven shortage and to special groups, like the elderly and disabled. The Institution considers that higher rents should operate in both public and private sectors, and that tax relief on mortgage interest might advantageously and equitably be restricted to the standard rate. They believe that a comprehensive overhaul of the system is urgently needed.

The main plank of Conservative housing policy is the sale of local authority houses to occupiers. This policy is not without its problems as most local authority houses were not built with eventual separation in mind; it could result in mainly the better built and located houses being sold and also operate to the disadvantage of tenants and those on waiting lists. Most would-be purchasers are likely to require large mortgages.

Some local authorities have suffered from very high maintenance bills for modern dwellings. This was highlighted in a Greater London Council housing report which contained an estimate of defects totalling £30 million on London housing estates. Many of the defects stemmed from the use of high-rise industrialised building systems. In an eight-year-old 201-flat development in Nottingham, it cost £600 000 to rectify damp penetration and defective brickwork. There is a need for greater attention to maintenance aspects at the design stage and for a representative of the housing department to be a member of the design team.

Much more attention should be paid to the costs and benefits of improving older dwellings to make more effective use of existing housing stock. The Dundee study[43] showed the application of cost–benefit analysis to this particular area and the Department of the Environment issued draft guidelines to local authorities using a similar approach in 1977.

Town and Country Planning

The separation of planning functions between county and district councils causes delays, duplication of resources and inter-authority disputes. The identification of county matters is often difficult. In addition, planning control is cumbersome and too wide-ranging, resulting in the submission of many planning applications relating to minor matters, whose impact on land use and the environment is minimal. Considerable simplification of the process is an urgent need, coupled with a clearer definition of the planning responsibilities of the two tiers of local government. The most bureaucratic aspect of reorganisation has been the proliferation of co-ordinating committees between the two tiers resulting in more staff and paperwork.

The Community Land Act 1975 had the twin objective of enabling the community to control the development of land in accordance with its needs and priorities, and of restoring to the community the increase in value of land arising from the development. Under the Act, local authorities will acquire land, whether for their own use or for private development, at current use value, but development gains are subject to development land tax. In the first year of operation, local authorities purchased over 1500 acres (600 hectares) at a cost of about £12 million.

Inner-city Renewal

The Prime Minister in early 1977 drew attention to the deteriorating situation in inner cities as a result of the exodus of people and industry. The Government was investigating ways in which it could best help city councils to remedy the situation and £100 million was included in the 1977 budget.

The Association of Municipal Authorities identified an urgent need for the renewal of the aging cores of industrial conurbations and considered that the two tiers of local government should pool their resources in order to prepare and implement the necessary programmes. The Association's report[44] recommended greater central government financial assistance, extension of the Community Land Act to provide powers for land assembly, reasonable compensation for derelict land, changes to the Industry Act to give help to inner-area firms and the inclusion of new factors in the rate support grant formula to ensure increased assistance to stress areas.

A report prepared by the Royal Institution of Chartered Surveyors[45] recommended that there should be an all-party commitment to solving the problems of inner-city obsolescence and decay, on a continuous basis and pursued with urgency. Local authorities are urged to assemble vacant land and acquire obsolescent areas, dispose of freeholds and grant leases of more than 99 years, initiate factory construction programmes and help with pump-priming finance.

Other Services

Considerable criticism has been levelled at the rapid expansion of local authority direct-labour building organisations in some areas. Ratepayers' organisations and private builders claim waste of resources, inefficiency and gross overspending. As with all technical staff, local authorities would be wise to keep a proper balance between public and private facilities.

In education, county councils have to face the demands of parents against a background of reducing funds. Reduced numbers of pupils in some age groups, less teacher training colleges, increased costs of higher education, replacement of old schools, the continuing demand for nursery schools and considerable opposition to comprehensive education all pose problems, at a time when the efficiency of the education system is being questioned. Certainly local education authorities should be given more scope to decide their own priorities. Furthermore, corporate management structures do not always operate in the best interests of the education service.[46]

Grimond[47] believes that the social services have expanded excessively and that the number of social workers should be reduced, with individuals doing more for themselves. Social services are organised by central government and hardly involve the community. Grimond recommends that the emphasis should be transferred from individual casework to work designed to prevent individual cases arising, accompanied by the provision of resources to the community.

The reduction of public expenditure is raising serious problems in the maintenance of highways and buildings. The deferment of maintenance expenditure is likely to aggravate defects with consequent increased expenditure later. Unless building repairs are carried out in time, the property may become damp or its structure deteriorate so that normal jobbing repairs and repainting are no longer sufficient to restore even an appearance of well-being.[48]

What of the Future?

The 1974 reorganisation of local government in England and Wales has not been without its critics. The present structure was formulated by the Conservatives, who were anxious both to retain and to strengthen the county councils at the expense of the former county boroughs, as much of their strength emanated from the counties. By direct contrast the Labour Party is keen to reduce the powers of the county councils and strengthen those of the larger urban areas for similar reasons.

There are evident defects in the 1974 structure, particularly in relation to the duplication and sharing of planning powers over the two tiers and the separation of housing and social services, which should ideally be closely integrated under the same authorities. It can also be argued, with some justification, that the county councils are too small for some functions, such as planning and transport, while the district councils are too large to deal effectively with grass-roots issues. The current system has thus resulted in some measure of fragmentation, overlapping, frustration, dispute and the waste of resources.

Having identified some of the main problems it is much more difficult to formulate effective and acceptable proposals to remedy them. To create larger authorities to administer planning and transport functions more effectively would involve the establishment of regional authorities, while the need for smaller authorities at grass-roots level could result in yet another tier of decision-making local government and further fragmentation, problems of communication and additional expense.

Many have sympathy with the larger towns and cities which have lost some important functions, such as education, highways, refuse disposal and libraries, to the county councils. Indeed the district councils' functions are quite restricted in scope, apart from their major activity of housing, and in so many issues they are dominated by the county council and this, in the absence of a high level of co-operation, can easily lead to friction and poor local government. A strong case can also be made for the concept of city regions as recommended by Derek Senior in his memorandum of dissent

to the Redcliffe-Maud Report, on the basis that the natural hinter-
lands, suburbs or environs of large towns and cities should form
part of their local government administrative areas, as the majority
of the residents tend to look to the town or city for their employment,
shopping and entertainment.

The separation of enlarged cities from the remainder of the country
leaves the less populated parts of counties occupying irregular and
inconvenient shapes and with much reduced resources. Such an
approach would also serve to sharpen the distinction between town
and country at a time when it is becoming increasingly recognised
that they are closely interdependent and should ideally be
administered as a single combined entity.

It is also apparent that the same solutions cannot be effectively
applied throughout the whole country, and this was recognised in
1974, when a separate structure was devised for the metropolitan
counties and districts. In like manner unitary authorities or city
regions might well be suited for some parts of the country but
not for others. The final plan must have regard to geographical,
social and economic characteristics of each area after identification
of local needs and aspirations.

There is considerable merit in retaining a two-tier system, each
tier having clear responsibilities, but incorporating a reasonable
measure of flexibility in its application, and endeavouring at all
times to secure the right balance between efficiency and democracy,
recognising that these are frequently in conflict. The author would
in general opt for a framework of regional authorities responsible
for such activities as transport, planning, education, fire and police.
District councils could be responsible for housing, social services,
recreation, libraries and public health matters. To overcome the
deficiencies at grass-roots level, neighbourhood councils could
perform a valuable role by identifying local needs and having
recognised links with the upper tiers of local government. In like
manner there is a need for a regional authority to co-ordinate matters
affecting London as a whole. Certainly the Greater London Council
is involved in far too many detailed issues which are better left
to the London boroughs.

It is very unlikely that any further major reorganisation could
take place before the 1980s because of the high cost and disruption
accompanying such a change. A wider-ranging reappraisal would
also be needed to embrace not only the present local authorities
and their areas and functions, but also central/local government
relationships, finance and the *ad hoc* water and health authorities.
A serious attempt should be made to reduce central interference
with local government and to widen the scope for local authority

initiative and action to identify and satisfy local needs and aspirations. The strengthening of democratic local government should be the aim of all patriotic politicians.

References

1. RICHARDS, P. G., *The Reformed Local Government System* (Allen and Unwin, 1975).
2. *Report of the Committee on the Management of Local Government* – the Maud Report (H.M.S.O., 1967).
3. STUDY GROUP ON LOCAL AUTHORITY MANAGEMENT STRUCTURES, *The New Local Authorities: Management and Structure* – the Bains Report (H.M.S.O., 1972).
4. NOTTINGHAM EVENING POST, 'Where your money goes – new councils: the staggering facts', *Nottingham Evening Post*, 30 August 1974.
5. BURKE, R., 'The murky cloak – any signs of light?', *Local Government Chronicle*, 21 and 28 June 1974.
6. KNOWLES, R. S. B., *Modern Management in Local Government* (Butterworth, 1971).
7. SCOTT, G., 'The Members' Information Service in the Greater London Council', *Local Government Studies*, January 1977.
8. HENDER, J. D., 'Services to members', *Public Finance and Accountancy*, 1, 10 (1974).
9. HOLDSWORTH, M., 'The other side of the Ombudsman', *Local Government Chronicle*, 21 January 1977.
10. SPORTS COUNCIL, *Planning for Sport* (Central Council of Physical Recreation, 1968).
11. SEELEY, I. H., *Outdoor Recreation and the Urban Environment* (Macmillan, 1973).
12. SPENCER, J. R., 'Dual schemes a reality', *Sports Development Bulletin*, No. 8 (Central Council of Physical Recreation, 1969).
13. FARRER, J., 'A modern approach to the provision of a sports centre: An example of co-operation between local authorities', *Proceedings of Conference on Planning for Management* (National Playing Fields Association, 1967).
14. SEELEY, I. H., *Planned Expansion of Country Towns* (George Godwin, 1974).
15. HARRIS, R. J. P., 'Inter-authority decision making – some implications for local government', *Local Government Studies*, July 1976.
16. DEPARTMENT OF THE ENVIRONMENT, *Making towns better* – the Sunderland Study (H.M.S.O., 1973).

17. BLESSLEY, K. H., 'London government 1965–77 through the eyes of a chartered surveyor', *Chartered Surveyor*, 109, 10 (May 1977).

18. *Report of the Royal Commission on Local Government in England 1966–1969* – the Redcliffe-Maud Report (H.M.S.O., 1969).

19. DEPARTMENT OF THE ENVIRONMENT, *Neighbourhood Councils in England* – consultative paper (H.M.S.O., 1975).

20. JACKSON, J., 'Roles for Neighbourhood Councils', *Municipal Review*, April 1977.

21. ROYAL COMMISSION ON THE CONSTITUTION – the Kilbrandon Report, Cmnd. 5460 (H.M.S.O., 1973).

22. DOUGLAS, J., 'The balance of power', *Local Government Chronicle*, 4 May 1973.

23. *Devolution within the United Kingdom: Some alternatives for discussion* – Government discussion paper (H.M.S.O., 1974).

24. CRAVEN, E., 'Regional devolution – the next steps', *Local Government Chronicle*, 21 June 1974.

25. HIMSWORTH, C. M. G., 'Our changing local democracy', *Local Government Chronicle*, 9 January 1976.

26. ASHFORD, D. E., 'Reorganising British local government: a policy problem', *Local Government Studies*, October 1976.

27. RHODES, R., 'The new politics of local government', *Local Government Chronicle*, 30 July 1976.

28. GYFORD, J., *Local Politics in Britain* (Croom Helm, 1976).

29. MALLABY, G., 'Sober and steady look at local government', *Local Government Chronicle*, 17 May 1974.

30. STEWART, J., 'Corporate control can only go so far', *Municipal Review*, March 1975.

31. BENINGTON, J., 'How Bains turned the elected member into a business executive', *Municipal Review*, March 1976.

32. KERSHAW, P. B., 'Political realities and local government', *Local Government Chronicle*, 21 February 1975.

33. SHARPE, D. E., 'Management services: friend or foe?', *Chartered Municipal Engineer*, May 1977.

34. SALMON COMMISSION, *The standards of conduct in public life* (H.M.S.O., 1976).

35. WELSH, L., 'Conduct in public life', *Journal of the Institute of Local Government Administrators*, 17, 6 (1976).

36. JONES, G., 'How to stay clean', *Local Government Chronicle*, 24 September 1976.

37. Cmnd. 6453, *Report of the Committee of Enquiry on Local Government Finance* – the Layfield Committee (H.M.S.O., 1976).

38. FREEMAN, R., 'False premises which bloat the public purse', *Municipal Review*, April 1976.

39. HICKS, U., 'The case for an easy end to spending', *Municipal Review*, April 1976.
40. LITTLE, B. ST L., 'A plea for unity', *Local Government Chronicle*, 10 December 1976.
41. STEVENSON, B., 'Local and central government relationships', *Public Finance and Accountancy*, October 1976.
42. ROYAL INSTITUTION OF CHARTERED SURVEYORS, *Housing: the Chartered Surveyors' Report* (1976).
43. GRANT, R. A., THOMSON, B. W., DIBLE, J. K. and RANDALL, J. N., *Local housing needs and strategies – a case study of the Dundee sub-region*, Scottish Development Department (H.M.S.O., 1976).
44. ASSOCIATION OF MUNICIPAL AUTHORITIES, *Cities in decline: Report on the problems of the old industrial cores of the metropolitan areas* (1976).
45. ROYAL INSTITUTION OF CHARTERED SURVEYORS, *Inner city regeneration – a report on some aspects of the inner city problem* (1977).
46. PRITCHETT, G. R., 'Municipal malaise', *Times Educational Supplement*, 12 November 1976.
47. GRIMOND, J., 'Individuals should do more for themselves', *Social Work Today*, 2 November 1976.
48. SEELEY, I. H., *Building Maintenance* (Macmillan, 1976).

INDEX